AN UNSETTLED ARENA

An
Unsettled
Arena

Edited by

WILLIAM B. EERDMANS PUBLISHING COMPANY

Religion
and the
Bill of Rights

Ronald C. White, Jr., and
Albright G. Zimmerman

GRAND RAPIDS, MICHIGAN

Copyright © 1990 by Wm. B. Eerdmans Publishing Co.
255 Jefferson Ave. S.E., Grand Rapids, Mich. 49503

Library of Congress Cataloging-in-Publication Data

An Unsettled arena: religion and the Bill of Rights / edited by
  Ronald C. White and Albright G. Zimmerman.
      p.   cm.
   ISBN 0-8028-0465-9
   1. Religion and state—United States. 2. United States.
Constitution. 1st-10th amendments. I. White, Ronald C.
(Ronald Cedric) 1939–   II. Zimmerman, Albright G., 1920–
BR516.U57   1989
322′.1′0973—dc20   89-27531
                                                         CIP

Contents

Acknowledgments

These papers grew out of a discussion at one of the Rider College Protestant Chaplain's Advisory Luncheons some three or four years ago. A lecture series was proposed and a committee that styled itself A Committee to Explore Religion and the Constitution was instituted. Every effort was made to incorporate a variety of views and a number of representatives of several constituencies into our committee. The committee meetings turned out to be enriching workshop sessions where bibliographies, articles, and ideas were exchanged as our suggestions developed into structured plans for the series of lectures. Each member of the committee subsequently acted as a moderator or commentator at one or more of the formal lecture sessions. Despite several retirements from the committee and several additions, each member has made positive contributions that helped to bring this volume to fruition.

Ultimately we prepared and submitted four separate grant proposals, all of which have been honored to varying degrees. We wish to recognize the two grants we received from the New Jersey Committee for the Humanities and the two grants we received from the New Jersey Historical Commission. Recognition should also be extended to the various institutions that became sponsors for our grants and for our series and also made further contributions: Rider College, Princeton Theological Seminary, the Presbytery of New Brunswick, and the Campus Ministeries of Trenton.

The result was seven lectures, five of which are included in this volume. These are supplemented by an additional lecture presented by Ronald C. White, Jr., for Rider College's Wilson Wismer Memorial Lecture Series and an introduction and epilogue prepared specifically for this volume by Albright G. Zimmerman.

The editors wish to recognize the following members of our committee:

Theodore W. Brelsford, Jr., now a graduate of Princeton Theological Seminary;

John H. Carpenter, Ph.D., Dean, School of Continuing Studies, Rider College;

David E. Collier, History Faculty, Mercer County Community College; former President, Trenton Historical Society;

William D. Guthrie, Ph.D., Associate Dean, School of Education, Rider College; former Moderator of Presbytery of New Brunswick;

Cynthia A. Jurrison, Ph.D. candidate, Princeton Theological Seminary;

Harvey R. Kornberg, Ph.D., Chair, Department of Political Science, Rider College;

Christopher P. Momany, now a graduate of Princeton Theological Seminary;

David Rebovich, Ph.D., Associate Dean, School of Liberal Arts and Science, Rider College; Political Scientist;

Nancy H. Schluter, Protestant Chaplain, Rider College, and former Chaplain at Mercer County Community College; now a graduate of Princeton Theological Seminary;

Louis A. Smith, D.S.T., former Chairman, Campus Ministries of Trenton; former pastor, Resurrection Lutheran Church, Trenton, New Jersey; now a teacher in a Lutheran Seminary in Namibia;

Ronald C. White, Jr., Ph.D., former Director of Continuing Education and Lecturer in Church History, Princeton Theological Seminary; now a fellow at the Huntington Library, San Marino, California;

Robert J. Williams, Ph.D., Pastor, First United Methodist Church, Pennington, New Jersey;

Albright G. Zimmerman, Ph.D., Chair, Department of American Studies, Rider College.

Each of the presentations in this volume is a statement made by the individual author and only by that particular author. The only exceptions are the contributions of the two editors, who did have the papers of the other contributors as they prepared their presentations. The editors would like to take this opportunity to publicly thank each of the participants.

We gratefully acknowledge the permission of *The Princeton Seminary Bulletin* to reprint the Wilson Carey McWilliams and Robert T. Handy lectures and of *This World* to reprint the Max L. Stackhouse article.

RONALD C. WHITE, JR.
ALBRIGHT G. ZIMMERMAN

Contributors

HARVEY COX is the Victor Thomas Professor of Divinity at the Harvard Divinity School. His religion courses are rated among the most popular on Harvard's campus. His books include *The Secular City; A Feast of Fools; The Seduction of the Spirit: The Use and Misuse of People's Religion; Religion in the Secular City: Toward a Post-Modern Theology;* and, most recently, *Many Mansions: A Christian's Encounter with Other Faiths.*

ROBERT T. HANDY is the Henry Sloane Coffin Professor Emeritus of Church History at Union Theological Seminary, where he also served as academic dean. Among his publications are *A Christian America: Protestant Hopes and Historical Realities; A History of the Churches in the United States and Canada;* and *A History of Union Theological Seminary in New York.*

WILSON CAREY MCWILLIAMS is vice chairman for undergraduate studies and professor of political science at Rutgers University. In addition to his highly regarded *The Idea of Fraternity in*

America, his numerous publications include a 1987 study of Tom Paine and civil religion in *Social Research*.

LEO PFEFFER is the former general counsel for the American Jewish Congress. He has argued more First Amendment cases before the Supreme Court than any other attorney. His books include *Church, State, and Freedom; Church and State in the United States; God, Caesar, and the Constitution; Religious Freedom;* and *Religion, State and the Burger Court*.

MAX L. STACKHOUSE is the Herbert Gezork Professor of Christian Ethics and Stewardship Studies at Andover Newton Theological School. He is a past president of the American Society of Christian Ethics. Among his books are *Apologia: Contextualization, Globalization, and Mission in Theological Education; The Ethics of Necropolis; Ethics and the Urban Ethos;* and *Creeds, Society, and Human Rights: A Study in Three Cultures*.

RONALD C. WHITE, JR., is a John Randolph and Dora Haynes Huntington Fellow at the Huntington Library, San Marino, California. He has served as faculty member or administrator at Rider College, Whitworth College, and Princeton Theological Seminary. His books include *The Social Gospel: Religion and Reform in Changing America; American Christianity: A Case Approach;* and *Partners in Peace and Education. Liberty and Justice For All: The Social Gospel and Racial Reform* (The Rauschenbusch Lectures) is forthcoming.

ALBRIGHT G. ZIMMERMAN is chair of the Department of American Studies at Rider College. He chaired the committee to explore the relationships between religion and the Constitution. He has published articles on colonial Pennsylvania, Indians, canals, and railroads.

Preface

Two hundred years after its creation, the Bill of Rights is an unsettled arena. The First Amendment, gathering dust at the beginning of this century as a memorial to a bygone era, today is the focus of public controversy and scholarly debate. An assortment of concerns—prayer in public schools, tax exemptions, the support of chaplains, aid to parochial schools, the teaching of creation, and the general inclusion of religion in public ceremonies—has aroused passions and precipitated discussions in communities across America.

A series of recent public events has highlighted the importance of the Constitution and the Bill of Rights. The bicentennial of the Constitution focused attention not only on its origins but on its contemporary meaning. The hearings to examine Robert Bork for the Supreme Court underscored the importance of the interpretation of the Constitution. Because these were the first such hearings to be televised, they became an opportunity for a civics lesson for many Americans. Even if the deliberations at times produced more heat than light, cases that were once the property of specialists became part of community conversations. The importance of the Bill of Rights was dramatized in the summer of 1988 with the signing of the Williamsburg Charter at historic Williamsburg, Virginia. Hailing "the genius of the First Amendment," the charter, signed by major political and religious leaders, calls for the positive role of religion in society, recognizing at the same time the need to "contend with each other's deepest differences in the public sphere."

While opinions differ widely, we can say with certainty that these debates and this contending will continue. It is not possible to return to an earlier, more homogeneous America. Pluralism will increasingly characterize America as the nation moves into the twenty-first century. At the same time, there is an increasing recognition that pluralism does not have to mean an absence of moral and ethical values. To deny the religious heritage of America in the name of pluralism lacks both hindsight and foresight. The specter of the Protestant Religious Right has sometimes worked to squelch honest dialogue about the best ways to insure that society recognizes the role of religion. We contend that the enormous problems facing our society can serve to bring thoughtful people together at the local and national levels in search of the best ways to express religious ideas and values in the public arena.

This volume is presented as grist for this continuing discussion. We offer it because we believe there is a need for light and not just heat. Since we recognize that to speak of "Religion and the Bill of Rights" intersects so many areas of society, our contributors represent a variety of both academic disciplines and practical experience. The authors are scholars in the fields of American studies, American history, church history, ethics, law, political science, and sociology. They have served in various ways in the intersection of church and society—arguing cases before the Supreme Court; lecturing in colleges and universities as well as divinity schools and theological seminaries; participating in official bilateral conversations between Roman Catholics and Protestants; and living and working in other cultures, thus bringing an international dimension to the conversation.

These contributors came together originally as lecturers for a series honoring the bicentennial of the Constitution. Their aim was to encourage vigorous discussion with citizens from all walks of life. In meetings that took place over eighteen months, people repeatedly focused their questions and concerns on the Bill of Rights.

We have compiled these lectures so that they can now be the basis of a continuing conversation. The year 1991 will mark the two hundredth anniversary of the Bill of Rights. In preparation for the events of that year, Professor Zimmerman and I hope that churches and synagogues, civic clubs, and classrooms will use this volume as a resource for their own discussion and action.

San Marino, California   RONALD C. WHITE, JR.

PART I: ORIGINS

The Religious Backdrop

Albright G. Zimmerman

The Bill of Rights, despite its hallowed status in the American hierarchy of our basic guarantees of liberty and freedoms, is apparently little understood by the citizens of our country, for they continue to take part in acrimonious disputes about its meaning. The arguments of such diverse opponents as the "pro-choice" and the "Right to Life" supporters, or of those who watched the television "spectacular" devoted to the nomination of Robert Bork, show that few people understand or agree on what the Bill of Rights actually guarantees. In these introductory comments I will examine and put into some perspective the bases for the principles that were ultimately incorporated into the pronouncement of rights, and will reconstruct the religious climate in which the framers of the Constitution and the authors of the first ten amendments operated. Too often the many misunderstandings within the public amphitheater of constitutional debate are characterized by a failure to understand the climate in which those amendments were created.

Modern interpreters of the Bill of Rights fall into several broad categories. During the 1950s, American society seemed to be rejecting its differences and instead seeking agreement or "consensus." For example, in his book *Protestant-Catholic-Jew,* sociologist Will Herberg argued that despite the quite different histories of these three traditions, in mid-century America they presented a united front that was overcoming past disunity. A major reason for this new unity was a common adherence to the religious values implicit in the American way of life. However, current proponents of civil religion have seen their role to be different and more sophisticated than was Herberg's.[1] According to sociologist Robert Bellah, American civil traditions became a higher reality that bound the traditional religions together in a consensus that superseded their differences—and incidentally defined the real American Mission. In a related analogous example, theologian Michael Novak has offered the interesting suggestion that the true religion of America is its commitment to its athletic spectacles.[2]

For many traditional Christians, the founding of America was achieved according to the providential purposes of God. In their eyes, therefore, the age of the Founding Fathers was one in which Christian virtue and devotion were universal. The new constitutional republic was a state that supported Christian institutions in general without favoring any single Christian establishment. The majority of those who call themselves Fundamentalists believe that prayer on public occasions and the laws that police the morals of the civil community (sometimes called "Blue Laws") are part of the American heritage, and that precedence validates the continuance of such public practices.[3]

1. R. Laurence Moore, *Religious Outsiders and the Making of Americans* (New York: Oxford Univ. Press, 1986), pp. 18-19; Will Herberg, *Protestant-Catholic-Jew,* rev. ed. (Garden City, N.Y.: Doubleday, 1960).

2. Moore, *Religious Outsiders,* p. 202; Jeffrey James Poelvoorde, "The American Civil Religion and the American Constitution," in *How Does the Constitution Protect Religious Freedom?* ed. Robert A. Goldwin and Art Kaufman (Washington, D.C.: American Enterprise Institute for Public Policy Research, 1987), pp. 143-49; Michael Novak, *The Joy of Sports: End Zones, Bases, Baskets, Balls and the Consecration of the American Spirit* (New York: Basic Books, 1976), *passim.*

3. For detailed consideration see *The New Christian Right: Mobilization and*

Apologists for a modern secular society, on the other hand, claim that the Enlightenment leadership was atheistic, an assumption that may have some validity for an eighteenth-century continental European *avant-garde*, although there is some basis to suspect the accuracy of even this proposition. But for eighteenth-century Britain and particularly for America, it takes some pretty extreme rationalization to equate the varieties of Natural Religion (sometimes called Deism), with their Christian overtones, with atheism.[4]

Even such early founders of the colonies as Roger Williams and William Penn are not spared misunderstanding by today's modern secular apologists, as well as by historical popularizers, who see them as intellectual, iconoclastic radicals in a twentieth-century sense. While Williams and Penn were thinkers who challenged the status quo in significant ways, neither endorsed a society with an absolute religious and social freedom that would tolerate any form of deviant social behavior or antisocial activities. What today's scholars fail to recognize is that societies of the eighteenth century and before were "organic" societies; that is, they saw themselves as intermeshed organic wholes in which the health of the organism required the suppression of any "abhorrent disease germs" that in any way threatened the whole. In 1825 an aged James Madison stated essentially the same assumption when he noted that there was a harmony between the facts of nature and the rational ways of "Nature's God."[5] More recently, in

---

Legitimation, ed. Robert C. Liebman and Robert Wuthnow (New York: Aldine, 1983), in particular: Jerome L. Himmelstein, "The New Right," pp. 13-30 (esp. pp. 16-19); Donald Heintz, "The Struggle to Define America," pp. 133-48 (esp. pp. 139-40); and James Davison Hunter, "The Liberal Reaction," pp. 149-63 (esp. pp. 160-61). See also James McBride, "'There Is No Separation of God and State': The Christian New Right Perspective of Religion and the First Amendment," in *Cults, Culture, and the Law: Perspectives on New Religious Movements,* ed. Thomas Robbins, William C. Shepherd, and James McBride (Chico, Calif.: Scholars Press, 1985), pp. 205-24.

4. Peter Gay, *The Enlightenment: An Interpretation,* vol. 2, *The Science of Freedom* (New York: Alfred A. Knopf, 1966), *passim;* Henry F. May, *The Enlightenment in America* (New York: Oxford Univ. Press, 1976), pp. 122ff., 167-70.

5. From Madison to Frederick Beasley, 20 November 1825, in *The Writings*

an article concerning religious liberty in Pennsylvania as evidenced in the 1776 and 1790 constitutions, J. William Frost has written:

> The revolutionary generation agreed that republican government required a virtuous citizenry, and a virtuous citizenry required morality, with religious observance the only sound ground for morality. The state, therefore, would pass laws that would help it remain unentangled from the institutional church, and would treat religious questions as issues of civil order and morality. The state justified legislation involving the churches on the basis of political and moral language. The government recognized that there should be a linkage between religion or moral language, but the state would keep its rationale for action to be morality, not religion. At the same time, the state and the courts would foster the observance of religion.[6]

William Penn, long an object of adulation, certainly is an example of an individual whose faith endured imprisonment and persecution and whose ideas of world peace and world government have branded him as being perceptive far beyond his time. For example, according to Thomas J. Curry, Pennsylvania was the only colony in which Catholics could worship in public. Yet a detailed examination of Penn's "Holy Experiment," the proprietary colony of Pennsylvania, reveals that as a socioeconomic reality, it was far less liberal than tradition would have it. In accordance with the beliefs of the Society of Friends, there was never a question of public support for churches or for tithes in the Quaker province. However, Penn assumed that "wildness and looseness of the People provoke the indignation of God," and he supported legislation outlawing swearing, drinking of healths, playing at cards and dice, stage plays, masques, and

---

of James Madison, ed. Gaillard Hunt (1904), 9:230-31, cited by Ralph L. Ketchum in "James Madison and Religion: A New Hypothesis," in *James Madison on Religious Liberty,* ed. Robert Alley (Buffalo: Prometheus Books, 1985), p. 176.

6. J. William Frost, "Pennsylvania Institutes Religious Liberty," *Pennsylvania Magazine of History and Biography* 112 (1988): 337-38.

cock fights, which would "excite the people to rudeness, cruelty, looseness and irreligion," a stand that would find a great degree of support in all of the colonies.[7]

In his reevaluation of Roger Williams's religio-intellectual positions, Edmund S. Morgan refuted the popularization of the Rhode Islander as a paragon of today's style of "religious liberty." In an analysis that brought dream back to reality, Morgan noted that Williams's "single-minded zeal in support of every cause he espoused has drawn attention away from the structure of his thought." Williams demanded freedom of conscience "because Christ demanded it," but he also believed, according to Morgan, that the conscience "belonged to the reason, and in vindicating it he was vindicating reason—reason corrupted by the fall of man, reason needing the aid of scripture and of saving grace but nevertheless, reason."[8] While Williams called for separation of church and state, his concern was to preserve the church from worldly contamination. At the same time, however, he believed that the state suffered when the church directed it away from its proper activities.[9]

Maryland's 1649 Act Concerning Religion, commonly referred to as the Act of Toleration, has been cited repeatedly as an example of religious freedom in early America. Actually, the Catholic Proprietors, faced by the realities of threats to the continued control of the colony, simply validated a situation already in place whereby both Protestants and Catholics could practice their religions freely. "Noe person," the act read,

7. Thomas J. Curry, *The First Freedoms: Church and State in America to the Passage of the First Amendment* (New York: Oxford Univ. Press, 1986), pp. 72-75; Gerard V. Bradley, *Church-State Relationships in America* (Westport, Conn.: Greenwood Press, 1987), pp. 46-49; for detailed analysis of Penn's various Frames of Government see Gary B. Nash, *Quakers and Politics: Pennsylvania, Sixteen Eighty-One to Seventeen Twenty-Six* (Princeton: Princeton Univ. Press, 1968).

8. Edmund S. Morgan, *Roger Williams: The Church and the State* (New York: W. W. Norton, 1987), pp. v, 142.

9. Morgan, *Roger Williams*, pp. 118-19; for a perceptive, brief analysis of Roger Williams, see Bradley, *Church-State Relationships*, pp. 27-30.

> professing to believe in Jesus Christ, shall from henceforth bee
> any waies troubled . . . for . . . his or her religion nor in the free
> exercise thereof . . . nor any way [be] compelled to the beliefs or
> exercise of any other Religion against his or her consent.

Yet, despite the fact that there was no tax-supported ministry
nor a required public worship, the law punished blasphemy
with death and forfeiture of property. Also prohibited was any
speech disrespectful to the Virgin Mary or the Holy Apostle, as
well as epithets denouncing the holders of any of seventeen
named religious viewpoints. As in most colonies, Maryland pro-
scribed punishments for profanation of the Sabbath.[10]

In 1652, during the Puritan Revolution, William Claiborne,
long an enemy of the Catholic Baltimores, led a contingent of
Puritans who seized control of Maryland and placed Puritan
forms in the forefront to the detriment of Catholicism. During
their subsequent restoration to power, the Baltimores uneasily re-
stored the precarious system of toleration. However, following
the Glorious Revolution of 1688, "toleration" was largely forgotten and in 1716 Catholics were disenfranchised in Maryland.[11]

Throughout the colonial period, there was a conviction that
government could not exist without religion, for without it there
would be no moral basis for society. Many agreed with the soon-
to-be provost of the College of Philadelphia, Anglican Dr. William Smith, who, in a letter to the *Mercury* in 1753, argued that

> *National Establishment* can alone diffuse . . . the full social Advan-
> tage arising from Religion and Men. . . . If . . . all Religions were
> equally favor'd by the Civil Power, none establish'd, and every
> Man left at Liberty to preach and practise what he thought proper,
> what a Scene of Confusion would thence arise . . . from such un-
> bridled Liberty of Conscience. . . . The Statesman has always

10. Curry, *First Freedoms*, pp. 39-41; Oscar Handlin and Lilian Handlin,
Liberty and Power, 1600–1760, vol. 1 (San Francisco: Harper & Row, 1986), pp.
64-65, 118; for even greater detail on restrictions on Catholics in Maryland, see
Bradley, *Church-State Relationships*, pp. 44-45.

11. Curry, *First Freedoms*, pp. 48-51; Patricia U. Bonomi, *Under the Cope of
Heaven: Religion, Society and Politics in Colonial America* (Oxford: Oxford Univ.
Press, 1986), pp. 21-24.

found it necessary for the Purposes of Government, to raise some one Denomination of religions above the Rest to a certain Degree.[12]

The Continental Congress noted that "true religion and good morals are the only solid foundation of public liberty and happiness."[13] Washington, in his Farewell Address, commented, "And let us with caution indulge the supposition that morality can be maintained without religion."[14] It was not moral man in immoral society, but rather immoral man in immoral society, and it was always necessary to provide a structure of laws that would protect sinful man from his own self.[15] Robert N. Bellah, in his landmark book, *Habits of the Heart,* noted that Gary Wills has called attention to the fact that the notion of public virtue was extremely important to the generation of the Founding Fathers, to whom it was not an abstraction but rather a visible quality exemplified by prominent men of the age. Bellah comments on the capacity in human beings

> to apprehend and pursue the good and to recognize in the character of others the qualities of integrity, grace, and excellence. Madison and his contemporaries thought of the pursuit of virtue as the way to reconcile the desire to be esteemed by one's peers with publicly beneficial ends.[16]

Bellah further noted that the Founding Fathers saw no need to "shape the political culture" of communities that had already shaped the religious, personal, and political orientation of their members.[17]

---

12. Quoted by Carl Bridenbaugh in *Mitre and Sceptre: Transatlantic Faiths, Ideas, Personalities, and Politics, 1689–1775* (Oxford: Oxford Univ. Press, 1962), p. 152.

13. Quoted by Curry in *First Freedoms,* p. 219.

14. *We Hold These Truths . . . : An Anthology of the Faith and Courage of Our Forefathers,* comp. Francis R. Bellemy (New York: Grosset & Dunlap, 1942), p. 65.

15. Terms borrowed from Reinhold Niebuhr's title, *Moral Man in Immoral Society* (New York: Charles Scribner's Sons, 1932).

16. Robert N. Bellah, Richard Madsen, William M. Sullivan, Ann Swidler, and Steven M. Tipton, *Habits of the Heart: Individualism and Commitment in American Life* (San Francisco: Harper & Row, 1985), p. 254.

17. Bellah et al., *Habits of the Heart,* p. 255.

Henry F. May, author of what is probably still the best work on the American Enlightenment, is very careful to note that the two most important ideas in colonial America were the Enlightenment and Protestantism. May characterizes his own study as being about the Enlightenment as Religion. In this light he observes:

> Men of the late eighteenth century, whether they were Calvinists or Arminians, deists or atheists, seldom thought about any branch of human affairs without referring consciously to some general beliefs about the nature of the universe and man's place in it, and about human nature itself. In this sense Jefferson and Paine were as religious as any New England Congregationalist. The denials and defiances of Enlightenment skeptics and materialists are denials and defiances of religious doctrine, usually religious in their own intent.[18]

How was this belief reflected in colonial Protestantism and in the Enlightenment? First, one must recognize that most colonial churches were strongly influenced by Calvinism. New England Congregationalists, Baptists, and Presbyterians simply practiced different forms of Calvinism, as did the Dutch Reformed and other Reformed congregationalists such as members of the German Evangelical and Reformed Church. Even the Virginia Anglicans who came from a pre-Laudian latitudinarian church were inclined toward Calvinism, as were many of the Methodists, particularly in America where George Whitefield's influence was felt. Calvinism emphasized a covenant theology that was reflected in the contractual nature of the corporate congregational church government. This was most obvious in the Anabaptist derivations such as the New England Puritans, the Baptists, and many of the German Reformed congregations, which practiced an independent congregational form of authority and governance. The response to the first query in the Shorter Catechism, "What is the chief end of man?" is, "Man's chief end is to glorify God and to enjoy him forever." In the attempt to implement Divine Will, policing the community "to glorify God"

18. May, *Enlightenment in America*, p. xiv.

became a duty incumbent upon all Christians. This was interpreted to mean that each believer must be his brother's keeper and that anything other than a moral society would be anathema to the deity. This injunction was also the basis for the Protestant virtues of frugality and hard work.[19]

No colony in America allowed absolute religious freedom, or for that matter personal freedom in the modern sense. Even proponents of "freedom of conscience" did not interpret this to mean full civil rights. Most supporters of this concept would in no way have restricted the civil government's right to police the morals of the community. Personal rights and privacy, to the degree that they were present and recognized, were largely limited to the right to engage in private practice of religion and little else. It might be useful to note that the Founding Fathers were repelled by the violence and demagoguery of the popular democracy of classical Athens. They took as their ideal the citizen of the early Roman Republic who subordinated himself to the discipline demanded by loyalty to the state and to its constitution.[20]

Furthermore, no colony legally permitted atheism. Until the passage of the Virginia Charter of Religious Freedom (1786), essentially composed by Jefferson in 1776 but not introduced in the Virginia legislature until 1779, no other colony had moved so far toward religious freedom. Yet even in the Virginia document, so praised by posterity, we read in Article 16 "that it is the mutual duty of all to practice Christian forbearance, love, and charity towards each other."[21]

19. "The Shorter Catechism," in *The Constitution of the Presbyterian Church (U.S.A.)*, Part I, *Book of Confessions* (New York: Office of the General Assembly, 1983), 7.001; see also "The Larger Catechism," 7.111; May, *Enlightenment in America*, pp. 44-48, 58.

20. See Forrest McDonald, *Novus Ordo Seclorum: The Intellectual Origins of the Constitution* (Lawrence: Univ. Press of Kansas, 1985), pp. 67-68; and see Federalist No. 10.

21. Cf. Curry, *First Freedoms, passim;* Charles B. Sanford, *The Religious Life of Thomas Jefferson* (Charlottesville: Univ. Press of Virginia, 1984), pp. 27-31; McDonald, *Novus Ordo Seclorum*, p. 43; Galliard Hunt, *The Life of James Madison* (New York: Russell & Russell, 1968), p. 8.

Although they had no established churches, New Jersey, Pennsylvania, and Delaware had tests for office-holding and voting. Even after the establishment of the federal government, Pennsylvania in its new Constitution of 1790 incorporated a section that "implicitly allowed Jews political rights. But the phraseology was such as to exclude atheists, pantheists, and animists."[22] It was by no means an open society, yet compared to most of their contemporary world, the degree of openness and freedom allowed in revolutionary America was excessive.

To summarize, what radical precedents were found in American colonial and revolutionary religious practices? In the writings of Calvin himself one can find the basic rationale for revolution. In his *Institutes of the Christian Religion,* Calvin affirmed that loyalty is due princes and magistrates, but when they are selfish, cruel, and evil, "consequently many cannot be persuaded that they ought to recognize these as princes and to obey their authority. . . ." The sixteenth- and seventeenth-century followers of Calvin and of the Calvinist doctrine of the "right of resistance" have been identified as the cause of many of Europe's religious wars.[23] In several of the colonies, particularly in Massachusetts, tax support was made available to more than one church (sect or denomination) as well as tax exemptions for dissenters, which in essence was a recognition of the right of various Protestant congregations to exist, something that was being denied in most areas of the world with established state churches. Even where there was establishment and no tax support for dissenting congregations, as was the case in many of the colonies, freedom of conscience was allowed, either by law or *de facto,* so long as one's religious observances were private and not public.[24]

22. McDonald, *Novus Ordo Seclorum,* p. 43n.

23. John Calvin, *Institutes of the Christian Religion,* 2 vols., ed. John T. McNeill, trans. Ford Lewis Battles (Philadelphia: Westminster Press, 1960), pp. 1511-12 (4.20.24); for an analysis of the Calvinist Puritans and revolution, see Michael L. Walzer, *The Revolution of the Saints: A Study in the Origins of Radical Politics* (Cambridge, Mass.: Harvard Univ. Press, 1965).

24. Leonard W. Levy, *The Establishment Clause: Religion and the First Amendment* (New York: Macmillan, 1986), pp. 1-25.

The notorious exiles and executions of Quakers in the Massachusetts Bay Colony in the early seventeenth century are examples of punishing individuals for their acts and not for their beliefs. After the new Massachusetts Charter of 1694, the Anglican Church, which was usually attended by British-appointed officialdom, and the congregations of dissenting Baptists and Presbyterians were tolerated and technically capable of being supported. Many colonies extended civil rights, that is, the right to vote and to hold office, to all believers, once property qualifications were met. In some cases merely belief in a Supreme Being was required, but more commonly the law required belief in the Christian Godhead, which was specified as Trinitarian. The latter provision was essentially the same as the requirements of the British Act of Toleration of 1689, which still disenfranchised Catholics and "other unbelievers"; however, colonial lawmakers often ignored this act.

After the Glorious Revolution of 1688-1689, William and Mary granted the British a Bill of Rights. Most of the new state constitutions of the revolutionary period also contained a Bill of Rights. What did all this mean as a background for the Constitutional Convention and the determinations concerning a Bill of Rights made during the first session of the new national Congress?[25]

The proviso in Article VI of the Constitution that there should be no test for office-holding constituted a decisive break with the past. While a degree of religious tolerance was present in virtually every colony, the qualifications for office-holding were stricter: higher levels of property-holding and religious requirements that concerned belief and often church membership.[26] The language of the First Amendment, which called for nonestablishment and freedom from government interference, was perhaps not startling in face of the struggles that had been going on in the various states, and certainly not in light of the

---

25. For a detailed catalogue of the situation in each of the colonies during the colonial period, see Curry, *First Freedoms, passim.*

26. Curry, *First Freedoms, passim.*

grim prognostications of the anti-Federalist opposition to the ratification of the new Constitution. In the eyes of the world, however, and in the eyes of most rulers and political philosophers, a state without the support of an established church could not long endure. Massachusetts would not erase the final vestiges of establishment until 1833.[27]

The Founding Fathers also achieved what most political theorists have called divided sovereignty. One of Britain's insoluble problems during the period preceding the American Revolution was Parliament's refusal to consider the possibility that the colonial assemblies could handle any degree of sovereign rights, or to recognize any portion of sovereign power residing in the colonial bodies politic.[28] Undoubtedly, this weighed heavily on the minds of the framers of the Constitution, who specifically granted carefully enumerated powers to the new national government while permitting the states to retain the balance of power. The states and the national government were each presumed to be supreme and exclusive in the exercise of their enumerated and retained powers. Each would deal directly with the citizenry in the implementation and enforcement of those powers. Apparently, this method has worked—as evidenced by two hundred years of successful constitutional government. Unfortunately, this division of power has been the basis for a continual struggle—a struggle to determine whether the allocations of absolute authority to the states and national government are still a reality in the twentieth century.[29]

27. Robert A. Rutland, "Framing and Ratifying the First Ten Amendments," in *The Framing and Ratifying of the Constitution,* ed. Leonard W. Levy and Dennis J. Mahoney (New York: Macmillan, 1987), p. 310.

28. Edmund S. Morgan, *Inventing the People: The Rise of Popular Sovereignty in England and America* (New York: W. W. Norton, 1988), esp. chap. 10, "The Incautious Revolution," pp. 239-62.

29. See Federalist No. 39, No. 51; McDonald, *Novus Ordo Seclorum,* pp. 276-84; John Patrick Diggins, *The Lost Soul of American Politics: Virtue, Self-Interest, and the Foundations of Liberalism* (New York: Basic Books, 1984), pp. 56-58; also Morgan, *Inventing the People,* pp. 264, 267, 270. I was first alerted to the conceptualization many years ago by a young French Canadian student leader who was concerned both by the nature of the National-Provincial governmental re-

The Constitution created in Philadelphia in 1787 was a document in line with the Enlightenment's ideas of contract theory and of natural law. In accordance with natural law, the framers assumed that the populace already possessed sovereignty and a body of rights. Thus, the new national government's powers would be limited to only those necessary to accomplish the ends specified, with the assumption that only those powers granted could be exercised. Viewed in this light, the Bill of Rights was a redundancy, but it was a political necessity in order to receive the support of those who feared a threat to the powers of the states.[30]

Madison and many of the strongest Federalists had opposed the idea of a Bill of Rights during the initial framing of the Constitution. They considered this to be the wrong path for the protection of civil rights, for they believed that further defining such rights might actually limit them. However, as we have noted, many of the state constitutions created during the previous decade had incorporated the device of a Bill of Rights. Further, the lack of a Bill of Rights became a pressing issue as the anti-Federalists quickly mounted an attack on the handiwork of the Philadelphia convention. One critic of the provision that denied any test for federal office, a member of North Carolina's ratifying convention, feared that not only might the new government deprive them of religious liberty but that in the absence of an appropriate test, "pagans, deists and Mahometans, might obtain offices." Such Federalists as Madison, Edmund Pendleton of Virginia, and Tench Coxe of Pennsylvania suggested that strategic support for the proposed amendments would rob the anti-Federalists of their best argument.[31]

---

lations in Canada and by the then still remaining remnants of British authority in the Commonwealth relations, a concept that is largely ignored by Americans but is possibly one that deserves greater concern with the growing imbalance between partners in our Constitutional arrangement.

30. Gordon S. Wood, *The Creation of the American Republic, 1776–1787* (Chapel Hill: Univ. of North Carolina Press, 1969), pp. 537-45; Morgan, *Inventing the People*, pp. 283-86; Levy, *Establishment Clause*, pp. 63-72.

31. Curry, *First Freedoms*, pp. 195-96.

In the debates at the North Carolina ratifying convention, someone asked why, if the new government guaranteed a Republican form of government, it did not also guarantee religious freedom? Federalist James Iredell responded to this query.

Had congress undertaken to guarantee religious freedom, or any particular species of it, they would then have a pretence to interfere in a subject they had nothing to do with. Each state, so far as the clause in question does not interfere, must be left to the operation of its own principles.[32]

In the Virginia debates, Federalist Governor Edmund Randolph responded with words that echoed Madison's Federalist No. 10 to Patrick Henry's fears that the powers of the new government without specific guarantees threatened religious freedom. After his general assertion that rebellion against England in defense of rights was not based on specific guarantees but that rights, at least by innuendo, had their bases in natural rights, he responded,

The variety of sects which abounds in the United States is the best security for the freedom of religion. No part of the constitution, even if strictly construed, will justify a conclusion, that the general government can take away, or impair the freedom of religion.[33]

Or, as one Federalist put it, "Why then should the people by a bill of rights convey or grant to *themselves* what was their own inherent and natural right?"[34]

Madison, as a result of political maneuvering by anti-Federalist Governor Patrick Henry, had to return to Virginia in 1788 to engage in vigorous electioneering against Henry's candidate James Monroe in an electoral district that had been redrawn in

32. "North Carolina: Excerpts from the Ratifying Convention, 1788," in *The States Rights Debate: Antifederalism and the Constitution,* ed. Alpheus Thomas Mason, 2d ed. (Oxford: Oxford Univ. Press, 1972), pp. 166-67.

33. "Virginia: Excerpts from the Ratifying Convention," in *The States Rights Debate,* p. 159.

34. From *The Documentary History of the Ratification of the Constitution,* ed. Merrill Jensen (Madison: State Historical Society of Wisconsin, 1976), 2:421.

an effort to deny Madison a place in the first House of Representatives. Madison placated the Baptist community with a promise that the Constitution protected the religious liberties of the citizens, "particularly the rights of Conscience." Madison pledged support for a Bill of Rights and communicated to his constituency that the way to procure the proposed amendments was through congressional initiation rather than through a second Federal convention. Despite a ten-inch snowstorm, Madison was successful on election day.[35]

In the new congress, Madison took the lead by proposing a list of amendments to the Constitution, including two relating to religion. The first called for the nonestablishment of any national church and the second applied restrictions against establishment on the states. The latter proposal was immediately dropped and not revived until the twentieth-century debates over the sway of the 1868 Fourteenth Amendment. After much debate in the House of Representatives and in committee, the final language for the amendment that also guaranteed freedom of speech and of the press was finally determined.

Numerous scholars have been concerned with exactly how the authors arrived at the final terminology.[36] Yet the seeming lack of critical but nonpartisan definitive works on religion and its continuing interaction with the Constitution is startling and appalling. The quantity of histories, commentaries, and polemics are awesome, but too often they are replete with sophistries, selective documentation, and deductive "truths," and present accounts are sadly lacking in the careful scholarship this author had hoped to find. Seemingly almost no work, except for an occasional article dealing with related topics such as the Enlightenment or Calvinism, and, in some cases, a biography, exhibit scholarship that rises above the petty and partisan. When researching the Founding Fathers, their understandings,

35. Rutland, "Framing and Ratifying," p. 308.
36. Discussions may be found in Donald L. Drakeman, "Religion and the Republic: James Madison and the First Amendment," in *James Madison on Religious Liberty*, pp. 231-47; Rutland, "Framing and Ratifying," pp. 305-16; and Levy, *Establishment Clause*, pp. 75-84.

and their intentions, it is unfair to take statements too literally and too often out of context and not to treat the spokesmen and participants as creatures of their age and of their own historical and ideological orientation. There have been far too many exegeses of the limited debates and too little attention to the history of the period. Further, the methodology used in many areas, particularly in the social sciences, is to deal with history from the point of view of what one scholar in another discipline calls "upstreaming"; that is, starting from the present and working backwards. While this may be rewarding when dealing with preliterate primitive societies, it should be used only with great circumspection when dealing with a society that started from so sophisticated a social and religious starting point as did the American.[37]

In Federalist No. 10 Madison indicated that the sheer size of the new nation guaranteed that there would be too many factions and interests for there ever to be a true majority that would exercise its tyrrany. He reiterated the same thesis in Federalist No. 51 where he noted,

> In a free government the security for civil rights must be the same as that for religious rights. It consists in the one case in the multiplicity of interests, and in the other the multiplicity of sects.

Recently, the American public was exposed to an entrancing television drama dealing with the nomination of Robert Bork as a Supreme Court justice. In some ways, the American public received an education in constitutional history; unfortunately, the lessons were too often clouded by the judgments of politicians. The public could have been better served by a program presented by historians and constitutional theorists.

Certainly one of the major concerns of the nation and of this book has to do with whether the changes wrought by technology—particularly those in the realm of the electronic media—altered the ground rules in such a way as to eliminate

37. William N. Fenton, "Huronia: An Essay in Proper Ethnohistory," *American Anthropologist* 80 (1978): 923-35.

that multiplicity of factions that Madison emphasized in Federalist No. 10. Or have the changes instituted by the Supreme Court's incorporation of the Establishment and Free Exercise clauses of the Bill of Rights into the Equal Protection and Due Process clauses of the Fourteenth Amendment and the homogenization of religion through the medium of Civil Religion erased the carefully structured division of power between the states and the federal government, which held so many implications for Americans to control their own communities and their institutions?

Religion and the
American Founding

Wilson Carey McWilliams

Celebrating the bicentennial of the Bill of Rights, we are apt to forget that the era of American founding was a time of uneasiness as well as confidence. A political founding demands daring, but entails dread: new laws open new pitfalls as well as new prospects. A political beginning is necessarily a venture into the unfamiliar, and the effort to create a new regime requires a turning from convention to theory, an appeal to first principles rather than second nature. The American framers observed the civil decencies in their speech and writing, but creating a new republic demands, at least, that one be willing to think shamelessly. Custom shrouds ambiguities and guards secrets, but political foundings ask us to envision things unclothed, as they are by nature.[1]

---

1. Thomas Pangle, "The Constitution's Human Vision," *Public Interest* 86 (Winter 1987): 78-79; Plato's *Republic* is the classic example of the relation between shamelessness and political founding. It is worth observing that in thought and in speech, the sin of Ham is apparently permissible, since Shem and Japheth were not punished for what they heard or imagined (Gen. 9:22-23). But the line is obviously delicate, especially since political founders translate thought

Americans found this sort of thinking uncomfortable because theorizing drew attention to the fundamental discord between biblical religion and secular rationalism, the antiphonies of American culture.[2] Then as now, most Americans felt some attachment to both traditions and preferred a downy equivocation to the discipline of dialectic. Yet willy-nilly, the logic of the founding imposed its own regimen, and Americans were forced to rethink the relation between religion and the new republic.

I

A great many Americans trusted or hoped that the new regime, while affording freedom of conscience, would be, at least implicitly, a Christian and Protestant commonwealth.[3] Prevailing Christian teaching, moreover, envisages a religious civility, a political order shaped by the principles of redemption and grace.

In that Christian understanding, the doctrine of redemption points toward the reconciliation of human beings with the order of creation—with nature, with their fellow humans, and with their own finite humanity. The incarnation attests to God's love for the world and proclaims that nature is lovable; Jesus' life reveals that human existence, with all its pains and imperfections, is touched by the divine, worthy of God's Son. For those who have conned its lessons, redemption teaches that we ought to strive to overcome human resentment against nature and its limits, saving life from the fury of human indignation: disciples

---

into action: a good political founding, in these terms, is necessarily a recovering of what has been laid bare.

2. Michael Kammen, *People of Paradox* (New York: Alfred A. Knopf, 1972).

3. See, e.g., the comments of the New Hampshire Anti-Federalist, "A Friend to the Rights of the People," in *The Complete Anti-Federalist*, ed. Herbert J. Storing (Chicago: Univ. of Chicago Press, 1981), 4.23.3, Remark 9; or Benjamin Rush, *The Letters of Benjamin Rush*, ed. L. H. Butterfield (Princeton: Princeton Univ. Press, 1951), 1:584, 611-12; and esp. Mercy Otis Warren, *History of the Rise, Progress and Termination of the American Revolution* (etc.) (Boston: Larkin, 1805), 1:17-18.

are the salt of the earth, meant to restore life's savor. The gospel liberates human beings by teaching them that nature's laws and limits are no bondage; redemption rejects the conquest of nature in favor of the mastery of self.

Political society was understood to play a crucial role in the secular education of the soul, and mainstream Protestant teaching regarded political life as natural and God-intended, necessary for human fulfillment. Indispensable as a restraint on vice, laws are also needed as a help to virtue: "A virtuous society cannot be happy without government," Joseph Lathrop wrote; "a vicious one cannot subsist without it."[4] Civil education should lead human beings out of self-centeredness into a broader sense of self as a part of the whole. And before we can learn to see nature as home-like, we need the experience of home; the effort to reconcile human with human requires laws that nurture and strengthen the bonds of community and the capacity for love. Public spirit, the foundation of secular civic virtue, is a step toward reconciliation with nature and, perhaps, toward Christianity's higher republic.[5]

By nature, Nathaniel Niles contended, there are no private rights. As Aristotle had observed, individuality presupposes the *polis*, a regime under which the division of labor permits each to do what he or she does best. Individual achievements, consequently, depend on the prior existence of political community, and private rights derive from public laws.[6] "Let our pupil be taught," Benjamin Rush urged, "that he does not belong to himself but that he is public property."[7]

Obviously, that doctrine wars against the Old Adam, and Christian theory insisted on stern laws to discipline and restrain

4. Charles S. Hyneman and Donald S. Lutz, eds., *American Political Writing During the Founding Era* (Indianapolis: Liberty Press, 1983), 1:659.

5. Samuel Davies, *Religion and Public Spirit* (New York: Parker, 1761); Gilbert Tennent, *Brotherly Love Recommended by the Argument of the Love of Christ* (Philadelphia: Franklin and Hall, 1748); Isaac Story, *The Love of Our Country Recommended and Enforced* (Boston: John Boyle, 1775).

6. Hyneman and Lutz, *American Political Writing*, 1:260-61; Aristotle, *Politics*, 1253a 19-20.

7. Hyneman and Lutz, *American Political Writing*, 1:684.

the passions. At the same time, it held that a good political society will entice the passions and draw the soul into the common life. Rightly governed, material delights and comforts help coax the soul out of the fortress of the self. Even a "Turk's paradise" of luxury, Gilbert Tennent argued, is better than the desire to be "a sort of independent being."[8] At a higher level, human capacities for love and friendship are strengthened by "exercise," just as they are undermined by self-seeking.[9] The best regime, consequently, encourages and honors the practice of civic friendship and public spirit.

Social stability, for example, makes it easier for us to know and trust our fellow citizens. Moreover, human beings will not run the inevitable risks of caring for others without some minimal assurance of *being* cared for: the laws must provide for the "particular care" which affords each child—and adult—the necessary evidence that he or she matters. Similarly, citizens will be more ready to invest themselves in public life when politics grants them dignity. Following ancient theory, Christian doctrine at the time of the founding was inclined to hold that the best political society is necessarily a small one, in which citizens know their rulers and are known by them, and in which individuals visibly can make a difference. In a small state, we can see and experience public benefits at first hand—our children attend new schools and we drive on new roads—but it is even more important that we have the chance to be heard on public questions or to listen if we prefer. In a large state, most of us are denied the choice between speech and silence, so that we assert our wounded dignity only by refusing to listen, confining our attention to that small, private sphere in which we matter.[10] Any

8. *A Solemn Warning to the Secure World from the God of Terrible Majesty* (Boston, 1735), p. 59, cited in Alan Heimert, *Religion and the American Mind* (Cambridge: Harvard Univ. Press, 1966), p. 306.

9. When human beings "neglect" the "exercise" of mutual love, Tennent wrote, they are inevitably "tempted, against the *Law of Nature,* to seek a *single* and independent state" (*Brotherly Love,* p. 3; his italics).

10. In a large republic where people have only a distant acquaintance with their representatives, the Anti-Federalist "Brutus" argued, "a perpetual jealousy

"vastly extended republic" can expect only a weak public spirit. Such a regime, consequently, stands in desperate need of the support and sanctions of religion; smaller states are more able to cultivate faith.[11]

Christian ideas of civic education included limits on the wealth as well as the size of political society. The division of labor frees talents and enriches civil life, but it can also divide society into competing interests and factions, each speaking a private argot. Since it is the whole that makes possible the specialization of the parts, in a good regime economics is kept firmly subordinate to politics. Wealth and the pursuit of wealth must be ruled by the public good: life must not become so cluttered or so complex that human beings lose sight of their dependence on one another and on the commonweal. "We must be willing to abridge ourselves of our superfluities for the relief of others' necessities," Winthrop told the Puritans, "having always before our eyes our commission and community in the work, . . . as members of the same body."[12] Even in private life, industry must be tempered by frugality, and a republic's citizens, thinking their liberties beyond price, must be willing to sacrifice well-being in favor of self-government. In principle, a good republic is small, simple, and austere, like the Christian Sparta for which Sam Adams hoped.[13]

It is worth emphasizing that Adams dreamed of a *Christian* Sparta: Protestant theorists might admire warrior virtue, but they rejected the closed community. In their view, it was part of the office of religion to remind citizens of their obligations to humanity, freeing public spirit from the reproach of xenophobia. The small republic is a necessary and desirable concession

---

will exist in the minds of the people against them: their conduct will be narrowly watched; their measures scrutinized; and their laws opposed, evaded or reluctantly obeyed" (*Complete Anti-Federalist*, 2.9.49; see also 2.9.18).

11. Hyneman and Lutz, *American Political Writing*, 2:1252.

12. "A Model of Christian Charity" (1630), in *Puritan Political Ideas*, ed. Edmund Morgan (Indianapolis: Bobbs Merrill, 1965), p. 92.

13. *The Writings of Samuel Adams* (New York: Putnam, 1908), 4:238.

to the "feebleness of human powers"; it must still be ruled by the higher law.[14]

In a similar way, even redemption derives from the ruling principle of grace. God's love is gracious because it is given freely and without condition, not because of merit but in spite of sin. Love, the royal law, is beyond justice, ignoring or sacrificing what is due the ruler in favor of the good of the ruled, insisting that the exalted must serve the lowly and treating the needs of the weak as obligations of the strong. The principle of grace, in other words, derives authority from the loving qualities of those who rule, not from the "consent of the governed."[15]

In a republic, this implies that the public spirit of citizens must rule their private interests and desires. Nathaniel Niles argued, for example, that a social contract founded for the mutual protection of private interests—the Lockean model of the origin of politics—is as much a usurpation as any tyranny, since it seeks to turn public things into private benefits. It changes nothing, in Niles' view, if a majority agree: numbers do not affect the question of right. Moreover, as Niles recognized, public-spirited citizenship often demands personal sacrifice and great courage, as when one defies the many. Even quiet law-abidingness must be willing to bear the burden imposed by the fact that some violate and many minimize their lawful obligations. The principle of grace, as Niles understood, prods citizens to do their duty without regard to reciprocities. In that sense, Christian citizenship ennobles republics by upholding a distinctly aristocratic ideal: "It is good, it is glorious to espouse a good cause, and it is still more great and glorious to stand alone."[16]

Love must be freely given and reconciliation must be agreed to: Christian teaching at the time of the founding re-

14. Hyneman and Lutz, *American Political Writing*, 1:263-64n.

15. E.g., rulers must, on the authority of Scripture, be persons who hate covetousness (Hyneman and Lutz, *American Political Writing*, 1:299-300, 434; 2:846, 1255).

16. Hyneman and Lutz, *American Political Writing*, 1:274; see also the extended footnote, 1:260-64.

garded liberty as an indispensable means to what is best in individuals and in politics. At the same time, Christian freedom denied that liberty is the highest—or even a proper—human goal: our natural rights are subordinate to what is naturally right, and the end is dutiful civility in a good regime. Love, after all, chooses to be ruled and to have duties, as Samuel Longfellow's hymn reminds us:

> Holy Spirit, Right Divine,
> King within my conscience reign.
> Be my law, and I will be
> Firmly bound, forever free.

II

The framers of the United States Constitution, by contrast, were informed by modern philosophies which held that, by nature, human beings are *free*, not political animals. Human nature, in this view, is defined by the body and its motions—human identity, Locke wrote, is "nothing but a participation of the same continued life . . . like that of other Animals, in one fitly organized body"—and our bodies are forever separate. We come into the world as we go out of it, alone: nature imposes no obligations and gives us no claims on one another.[17]

Human beings are naturally moved by their passions, and especially by the desire for self-preservation, a "fundamental, sacred and unalterable law," Locke argued, prior to revelation or reason and the "first and strongest desire God planted in men."[18] Nature, however, frustrates and ultimately kills us. It does not matter whether nature is hostile, indifferent, or the work of a benign Artificer who intends to inspire us to effort: by nature, human beings are driven to master nature. Humankind,

---

17. *Essay on Human Understanding*, Book II, chap. 27, sect. 6. "There is no other act of man's mind . . . naturally planted in him," Hobbes maintained, "but to be born a man and live with the use of his five Senses" (*Leviathan*, chap. 3).

18. *Treatises of Government*, I, sect. 86, 87; II, sect. 149.

Hobbes had it, is moved by "a perpetual and restless desire of power after power that ceaseth only in Death," and that pursuit of dominion is humanity's only truly natural end.[19]

It follows, of course, that the human struggle to triumph over nature precludes any reconciliation with it. Accordingly, when the framers speak of the divine, they often refer to the Creator, but never to the Redeemer. Their modern teachers urged the framers to regard the doctrine of redemption as a prescription for surrender, virtual treason to the human cause.[20]

Modern political science, in the eighteenth century, was no more friendly to the principle of grace. Natural freedom implies that human beings are rightly bound only by their consent. Authority does not derive from or depend on the qualities of the ruler: it is the creature of the ruled, the creation of their agreement and contract.

In the framers' understanding, political society is made or contrived by naturally free individuals in order to further their essentially private purposes—especially the "taste for property," or so Gouverneur Morris told the Convention.[21] In the familiar locutions of social contract theory, we "give up" certain natural rights in order to enjoy more effectively those we retain. The public good is only the aggregation of private goods; political society does not exist to make us alike, but to preserve our differences. Protecting "diversity in the faculties of men," Madison asserted, is the "first object of government."[22]

This view of politics establishes a *prima facie* case for a large and affluent state, able to enhance diversity and individual freedom through a more elaborate division of labor and capable of amassing power for the fulfillment of human desire and the conquest of nature. The framers recognized that smaller regimes promote the strong bonds of civic friendship and patriotism,

19. *Leviathan*, chap. 11.

20. Catherine Albanese, *Sons of the Fathers: The Civil Theology of the American Revolution* (Philadelphia: Temple Univ. Press, 1976), pp. 112-42.

21. James Madison, *Notes of Debates in the Federal Convention of 1787* (Athens: Ohio Univ. Press, 1966), p. 244.

22. Federalist No. 10.

which in turn are apt to prompt political daring and human excellence. They conceded that, in a large republic, sentiments of solidarity will be "diffuse" and probably will be outweighed by private loyalties and interests. But remembering the persecutions and disorders of Europe's recent past, the framers held that strong convictions, in politics or religion, are apt to produce turbulence and oppression. The ancient city-states, Hamilton wrote, produced "bright talents and exalted endowments," but these human achievements were "transient and fleeting," tarnished and misdirected by the "vices of government" with which they were associated.[23] Hamilton would have applied his remark to Jerusalem as readily as to Athens; the framers' ideal was a commercial republic, not a sacred city.

Nevertheless, the framers believed, as had Locke, that political society needs the support of religion. Religion inculcates the decencies: a powerful help in the government and moral instruction of children, it is also indispensable in establishing the duties of parents.[24] Moreover, religion is a buttress for law-abidingness among the ruled, for whom the advantages of right conduct are not apt to be immediately evident.

Liberal political philosophy, in the tradition of Hobbes and Locke, had no difficulty in demonstrating that self-interested human beings, exposed to the insecurities of the "state of nature," have every reason to make the promises necessary to create civil society. Once civil order has been established, however, the reasons for keeping one's promises are much less compelling. In fact, self-seeking individuals are bound to conclude that, in theory, it is desirable to be able to break one's promises while one's fellows keep theirs, reclaiming one's natural liberty while enjoying the advantages of civil society.

23. Federalist No. 9.
24. Nathan Tarcov, *Locke's Education for Liberty* (Chicago: Univ. of Chicago Press, 1984). While natural reason does indicate some responsibility toward what one has begotten, Locke pointed out, it did not prevent the practice of infanticide among the civilized ancients (*The Reasonableness of Christianity*, ed. I. T. Ramsey [Stanford: Stanford Univ. Press, 1958], sect. 242). Children have even less obligation toward their parents, since they have not consented to parental rule.

These calculations, however, are far more plausible in the case of great and prominent persons—who are likely to be noticed and emulated—than they are in the case of private citizens. This is no small problem since, as Hamilton observed, the spirit of enterprise is "unbridled" and strains against all restraint.[25] The liberal response is least persuasive when addressed to those who are obscure and unpropertied, who may calculate that their conduct is all too likely to go unnoticed. The framers knew well enough that the poor and the desperate—and in America, the enslaved—may easily come to feel that they have nothing to lose. Locke concluded that "promises, covenants, and oaths," the basis of civil society, stood in need of religious sanction. "The taking away of God, though but even in thought, dissolves all."[26] And even Jefferson wondered whether an atheist's testimony could be accepted by a court of law.[27]

Religion was also needed, in the framers' judgment, to support broader interests—the claims of society as a whole or of humanity—against narrowly private concerns. Reason and humanitarian feelings may touch us, but they are unlikely to prevail against bodily desires or the pressures of our immediate, day-to-day relationships. Jefferson did not doubt that slavery was a violation of natural right; he knew, however, that slaveholders would rate their investment in slave property above their more abstract interest in human liberty, unless religion could tip the scale.[28]

"Had every Athenian citizen been a Socrates," Madison wrote, "every Athenian assembly would still have been a mob."[29] He was contending that Socrates took a high moral tone because his public role made him visible and liable to praise and blame. In an assembly of philosophers, however, those in the back rows,

---

25. Federalist No. 7.

26. *Letter Concerning Toleration* (Indianapolis: Bobbs Merrill, 1982), p. 52.

27. *Notes on the State of Virginia* (Chapel Hill: Univ. of North Carolina Press, 1955), p. 159.

28. *Life and Selected Writings of Jefferson*, ed. Adrienne Koch and William Peden (New York: Modern Library, 1944), pp. 570, 639-40, 703-4.

29. Federalist No. 55.

feeling themselves less apt to be noticed, would not be able to keep themselves from talking to their neighbors or behaving like rowdies. Madison's precept implies that rulers—caught up in the broader world, honored when public policy succeeds and subjected to opprobrium when it does not—can be expected to give serious attention to the common good. Private citizens, however, naturally must be expected to follow their private interests, defined in more or less parochial and short-sighted terms. And obviously, in a large republic, only a tiny fraction of citizens can participate in ruling in any way other than voting. The framers, consequently, were inclined to seek religion's help in upholding patriotism and enlightened self-interest among the ruled.

In addition, the framers had very special reasons for seeking an accommodation with Christianity. Prudence taught them that it is politically dangerous to combat deeply-held beliefs, and most of the framers were convinced that a purely rational religion, like the Deism to which so many of them were attracted, would be inadequate for children, as yet not rational enough to appreciate it, or for those whose rational interests furnished only uncertain support for civil order—preeminently the poor, women, and slaves. And in some ways, the framers approved of Christian teaching. For example, they applauded and appealed to Christianity's proclamation that all human beings are members of one family, regarding Christian universalism as more comportable with reason than narrowly national religions like Judaism (in the framers' very distorted understanding).

The framers would not accept a détente with Christianity, however, until they were persuaded of their ability to curb Christian *political* teaching, averting or neutralizing Christianity's tendencies to fanaticism and its desire to elevate the soul. The framers hoped, as Locke had, to discipline Christianity, civilizing it down to a support for a liberal regime.

Forced to deal with an established church, Locke had set down his own theology, a "reasonable" Christianity which deemphasized or denied the doctrines of redemption and grace. Locke's creed proclaims Christ as the Messiah, a triumphant

King who overcame death and, hence, an inspiration in the struggle to master nature. He rejects the idea of Jesus as the Son of Man, the suffering servant who assumed, and showed the nobility of, human life and its burdens.[30] Second, Locke's Christianity emphasizes a "good life according to virtue and morality," which, in Locke's view, could be satisfied by observing the secular decencies.[31] In fact, Locke rejects virtually any *political* application of Christian teaching. In the *Letter Concerning Toleration,* for example, he denies that charity ought to influence law, asserting that politics should limit itself to safeguarding public peace and protecting "men's rights."[32]

Many of the framers shared Locke's doctrine and more regarded it sympathetically, but they regarded it as unnecessary in America. Lacking an established church, America did not need a civil theology. Civil religion could be embodied in laws and institutions like those Locke had prescribed, denying official standing to any religion, at least at the national level, and relying on the multiplicity of sects to check and confute any par-

30. E.g., discussing Mark 8:35-38, Locke says that the punishment for those who would not follow Jesus was "to lose their souls, i.e., their lives" (*Reasonableness of Christianity*, sect. 15). The passage, of course, suggests that human beings ought to lose their lives, "for my sake and the gospel's," in order to save them. Locke claims that the meaning of the passage is "plain, considering the occasion it was spoken on." But that occasion involves a rebuke to Peter, who, like Locke, proclaimed Christ the Messiah and denied that "the Son of Man must suffer many things" (Mark 8:29-31). Locke implies, however, that Jesus rebuked Peter as part of his "wise and prudent" effort to deceive the authorities about his intent (*Reasonableness*, sect. 59, 61, 139). Locke's argument also points to the conclusion that Jesus eventually bungled this alleged strategy.

31. *Reasonableness*, sect. 16, 67, 70-72, 167, 171-72, 179-80.

32. *Letter Concerning Toleration*, pp. 30, 42; early in the *Letter*, Locke cited Luke 22:25-26, 2 Tim. 2:19, and Luke 22:32. This amounts to a subtle editing that substitutes 2 Tim. 2:19 for the omitted passages from Luke, the second halves of verses 25, 26, and 32, and all of verses 27-31. These omitted verses suggest a hierarchy of regimes: they assert that among the unfaithful Gentiles, *any* lordship is a "benefaction," while the disciples, among whom equality is the rule, have a right to judge the law-abiding Tribes of Israel. Any form of rule is better than lawlessness; law is higher than lordship; equality is the rule for human governance informed by grace. Locke rejects this somewhat radical and very exacting standard in favor of the more limited demands of 2 Tim. 2:19.

ticular creed.[33] Thus limited—and even before the First Amendment to the Constitution ruled out any religious test—Christianity and all other religions could be left to their own devices as part of the private sphere.

This familiar solution, however, is less neutral than it may seem to be. Locke's philosophy suggested that the mind naturally follows experience. On that assumption, the laws, by establishing rules of practice, gradually will also establish a variety of civil theology. The framers designed a liberal and commercial republic, opened to the marketplace of ideas as well as of economics. Confronted with competing ways and views, Americans—the framers were confident—would become less and less inclined to give all their allegiance to any. Over the long term, Americans would insist on their individual right to judge creeds, seeing doctrines and teachings as analogous to commodities for sale. And the framers expected that the accepted standard of value would come to be liberty, the ability to do as one wills, enhanced by an increasing command of nature.[34]

III

Religion, of course, has proved to be stronger and more durable than many of the framers expected. Biblical political ideas, especially in their Christian articulations, have exerted a powerful force and spell in the life and thought of the republic.[35] In part,

33. Hyneman and Lutz, *American Political Writing,* 1:632-33; *Notes on the State of Virginia,* p. 161; Harvey C. Mansfield, Jr., "Thomas Jefferson," in *American Political Thought,* ed. Morton Frisch and Richard Stevens (New York: Scribner's, 1971), p. 38; *Letter Concerning Toleration,* pp. 13, 15, 19, 25, 27-29, 52, 54-55.

34. Sanford Kessler, "Jefferson's Rational Religion," in *The Constitutional Polity,* ed. Sidney Pearson (Washington, D.C.: Univ. Press of America, 1983), pp. 58-78; Thomas Pangle, *Montesquieu's Philosophy of Liberalism* (Chicago: Univ. of Chicago Press, 1973). For a contemporary statement of the same thesis, see Claude Lévi-Strauss, *Totemism* (Boston: Beacon, 1963), p. 89.

35. See my essay, "The Bible in the American Political Tradition," in *Religion and Politics,* ed. Myron Aronoff (New Brunswick, N.J.: Transaction, 1984), pp. 11-45.

this is due to the intrinsic merit of biblical teaching, which knows the soul and speaks to the human condition more profoundly than does modern secularity. It is also the result of religion's attention to that shaping of the "first impressions of the mind" which Benjamin Rush prescribed as a protection against indifferent or hostile laws.[36]

Nevertheless, as Robert Bellah and his associates contend, the "habits of the heart" are waning under the influence of the laws. Even where their conduct is influenced by better principles, Americans are more and more apt to speak the language of individualism, whether they appeal to a utilitarian calculus of self-interest or to the expressive individualism of authenticity and "what is right for me."[37] Americans seem to be losing the ability to speak and think in that language of grace and redemption which has been the counterpoint to liberalism in our national composition.

We cannot do without that second voice in our public forums. In its third century, the republic will require more than individualism and self-seeking; constitutional democracy will call for high citizenship and great consecration. Our debts demand financial sacrifice; equal justice and civil order oblige us to curb our passion for individual rights and private liberties; the pursuit of peace binds us to risk both lives and freedom. In these stern duties, there is also a thundering political vocation, and our biblical heritage can remind us that even those who are in the wilderness may have an engagement at Sinai.

36. Hyneman and Lutz, *American Political Writing,* 1:680, 683; *Letters of Benjamin Rush,* 2:947, 1075.
37. Robert Bellah et al., *Habits of the Heart: Individualism and Commitment in American Life* (Berkeley and Los Angeles: Univ. of California Press, 1985).

PART II:
BETWEEN THE TIMES

The Trajectory of Disestablishment: Public and Private Religion in America

Ronald C. White, Jr.

The religious revival of the 1970s and 1980s has elicited a reassessment of the state of religion in America. This broad-based renewal has challenged the predictions that America was entering a new secular age. First to catch the public's attention was the upsurge of self-conscious "evangelicalism." But a second look has revealed a pursuit of everything from the ancient religions of Asia to the "New Age" movements. We see now that this new interest in things spiritual has been accompanied by a dramatic decline in the so-called mainline churches (American Baptist, Episcopal, Lutheran, Methodist, Presbyterian, and United Church of Christ [Congregational])—so much so that we are beginning to call them the oldline churches.

The hallmark of this religious revival is a concentration on the personal dimension of faith. In 1976 Martin Marty spent thirty-eight weeks tramping around the country speaking on the Bicentennial. Asked in a radio interview about what he had learned from that year, he reported that he had found a great deal of interest in private or personal faith, but not much enthusiasm for expressing that faith in the public arena. The

37

churches that are growing emphasize the benefits to the individual.

This foreground is the vantage point from which to ask some questions about the trajectory of disestablishment. As the bicentennial of the Constitution was observed in 1987, much of the discussion of the First Amendment centered around the question of the original intent of the authors. One side argued that a proper understanding of the "Establishment Clause" in the First Amendment meant that there could be no aid of any kind to religion. They cited Thomas Jefferson and James Madison and the debates in Virginia to argue that even nonpreferential aid is to be prohibited. The other side argued that the framers of the Constitution and Bill of Rights were concerned to prohibit a national religion. The problem, this side said, was preference. They pointed out that after the First Amendment the federal government and the states continued to support and assist religion in a variety of ways.

In this chapter we will explore not the intent but the implications of the First Amendment. While it will be necessary to speak of intentions, our task is not to analyze the philosophy or grammar of the amendment but to explore its effects and thus its significance.

In approaching this task I am addressing a question that has been energizing much of my own reflection about religion and the Bill of Rights: Did the act of disestablishment set in motion a trajectory that led inevitably toward the privatization of religion in America? By "trajectory" I mean to convey a sense of direction in which there are zigs and zags. The trajectory is sometimes hidden from view, for example by the power and scope of the nineteenth-century voluntary societies or the twentieth-century civil rights movement. Nevertheless, the trajectory toward private religion has continued; some would argue that it is even more evident in our own day.

I propose to examine this trajectory in three stages. First, let us look briefly at the meaning of establishment in the colonies and the response of the new nation to disestablishment. Second, I will focus on some developments in nineteenth-century

American history and religious life that fostered individualism. Third, I will make some observations about the present status and shape of the trajectory toward personal religion.

I

In this bicentennial year of the Bill of Rights it is a worthy exercise for all citizens of this republic, and especially for members of religious communities, to try to understand the intention and implications of disestablishment. In recent years the sometimes heated debates about the so-called separation of church and state have clouded our comprehension of what disestablishment was intended to prevent and what it was intended to preserve.

Our understandings will be better informed if we remember the contours of establishment at the time of the American Revolution. In 1771, Thomas B. Chandler, an Anglican minister in New Jersey, wrote to Charles Chauncy, the venerable Boston Congregational divine, chiding him on continually changing the meaning of the word *establishment*. Chandler suggested that Chauncy publish a glossary where the different definitions might be explained.[1] Chauncy was merely referring to the different meanings of establishment as currently defined in the colonies.

There was no consistency among the colonies in this area. In Massachusetts and Connecticut, people who had been for the most part dissenters in England founded the established churches of New England. But these Congregationalists, despite the lingering mythology about their establishing a theocracy, sometimes had to tread lightly. Even though the Congregational Church was by far the largest church in the two colonies, there was always the fear that the English government, prodded by

---

1. Thomas J. Curry, *The First Freedoms: Church and State in America to the Passage of the First Amendment* (Oxford: Oxford Univ. Press, 1986), pp. 105, 127-29.

the established Church of England, might interfere. In New York, the Anglican Church was established in five counties in the southern part of the colony, even though it was a minority church in terms of numbers. The Church of England was also established in Maryland, Virginia, the Carolinas, and Georgia. All residents were taxed, but office-holding was not confined to Anglicans. New Jersey, Pennsylvania, Delaware, and Rhode Island established no religion. The decentralized system that developed in New Hampshire meant that local towns handled their own religious affairs.

It is worth recalling at this point how much the experience of establishment intruded from across the Atlantic. The memory of establishment, in England and elsewhere, was very much alive. In England establishment meant the Church of England, which at the time of the Revolution probably accounted for more than 90 percent of the population. The government approved of the church and supported it financially. In the American mind the tyranny of king was associated with the tyranny of bishops.

* * *

During the four months of the Constitutional convention of 1787 the delegates did not formulate a Bill of Rights. They believed that such an enumeration would be superfluous because the new federal government possessed a limited function. To begin to list rights would be to make a presumption about powers that the government should not have in the first place. As for religious rights, most Americans believed that the question of religion could be left to the states.

As the convention was drawing to a close, George Mason of Virginia suggested the need for a federal Bill of Rights. A motion to create a committee to prepare such a bill was defeated by a unanimous vote. But the wisdom of the framers of the Constitution, affirmed on most measures, was soon challenged in the ratification process. As the state conventions were considering the Constitution, many expressed a strong concern about the absence of a Bill of Rights. By 1789 bills of rights would be written into eight state constitutions. Criticisms were intense in Massachusetts and Virginia, and North Carolina went so far as to say that its ratification was tied to an early adoption of a national Bill of Rights.

At the first session of the first Congress, on June 8, 1789, James Madison proposed the addition of amendments to the Constitution. In the face of apathy and opposition, Madison argued that all power is subject to abuse and therefore requires safeguards for "the great rights of mankind." A conference committee of the two houses of Congress finally agreed to the ten amendments, but credit for the wording of the First Amendment belongs entirely to Madison. The House accepted the conference report on September 24, 1789, the Senate a day later.

After a remarkably brief debate, the First Amendment was accepted. In final form it reads:

> Congress shall make no law respecting an establishment of religion, or prohibiting the free exercise thereof; or abridging the freedom of speech, or of the press; or the right of the people peaceably to assemble, and to petition the government for a redress of grievances.

The movement for disestablishment was meant to prevent the kind of dominance enjoyed by the Church of England in England. This memory lay behind the first clause: "Congress shall make no law respecting an establishment of religion. . . ." The lesson learned from history was that establishment did not deal simply with religious dominance, but went hand in hand with political dominance.

Disestablishment was meant to preserve the vitality of religion by a structure allowing parity among churches. Although the second clause of the First Amendment ("or prohibiting the free exercise thereof") seems to be cast in the negative, its intention is wholly positive. The movement for disestablishment presumed the vitality of religion, which was understood at the time to be Protestant or Evangelical (the words were used almost interchangeably through the nineteenth century), which accounted for the majority sentiment of the people. Even those founders of the American experiment who were Deist appreciated Christianity because of the agreed-upon need for a religious basis for ethics and morals in society.

*   *   *

It is worth remembering the changes in attitude wrought in just a generation. Many are surprised to learn that establishment did not disappear all at once. New York did away with establishment in 1777. Under Thomas Jefferson's urgings, the Anglican Church lost its establishment in Virginia in 1785. But the two bulwarks, Connecticut and Massachusetts, where the populace identified the Congregational Church as the church of the patriots, did not undo establishment until 1817 and 1833 respectively.

As disestablishment was imminent in Connecticut, Lyman Beecher, prominent Congregational minister, preached with energy against it. When disestablishment came in 1817, Beecher experienced a severe depression. But he quickly recovered! Years later he looked back and said: "It cut the churches loose from dependence on state support. It threw them wholly on their own resources and on God."[2] Indeed, Andrew Reed, a Scottish minister who traveled to the United States in 1835, afterward wrote that he could not find one American minister who opposed disestablishment.

Why this change of heart? Because Beecher and others were participants in a new establishment of religion rooted in a mighty phalanx of voluntary societies. In the euphoria of the celebrations of the bicentennials of the Declaration of Independence in 1976 and the Constitution in 1987, many forgot that the good old days of Revolutionary America were not always so good for religion. With energies directed toward political questions and military battles, church attendance dipped markedly. Many local pastors went off to war as chaplains. Church membership, which admittedly was more strictly defined by stan-

2. Lyman Beecher, *Autobiography*, ed. Charles Beecher (New York: Harper and Brothers, 1864), 1:344.

dards of belief, experience, and behavior, was between 5 and 10 percent of the population in 1776.

Disestablishment in Connecticut and Massachusetts occurred in the midst of a religious renewal that helped transform the new nation. Revivals contributed enthusiastic volunteers to local and national voluntary societies concerned with Bible, book, and tract publications; foreign and home missions; education; and a variety of reform causes, including abolitionism, temperance, peace, and women's rights. Ministers were especially influential in this awakening in the new nation; as Lyman Beecher observed, "by voluntary efforts, societies, missions, and revivals, they exert a deeper influence than ever they could by queues, and shoe-buckles, and cocked hats, and gold-headed canes."[3] The successes of what came to be called the Second Great Awakening seemed to silence any discussion of the First Amendment.

II

But things are not always what they appear to be. Frenchman Alexis de Toqueville, who visited the United States in the 1830s, has an appropriate analogy. He tells of a traveler ascending a hill outside a large city. At the beginning of his climb he focuses on individual houses, streets, and people. Toward the top of the hill most of the individuality is gone but for the first time he can see the city whole.

For all of Lyman Beecher's prophetic insight about the future of America, he was unable to imagine what a different nation would emerge in the century after disestablishment. The revivals and voluntary societies gave promise of producing a united society undergirded by an evangelical ethos. Unfortunately, there was a shadow side to this vitality. Several dimensions were developing in America that would hasten the day of private religion. We will discuss three of these dimensions briefly.

3. Beecher, *Autobiography*, 1:344.

The first dimension was the focus within American revivalism on personal experience. Whereas the Calvinism that underlay Puritanism focused on a theology of the covenant that emphasized horizontal as much as vertical commitments, revivalism came to focus more on a direct, personal experience of God in Christ. To put it another way, if Jonathan Edwards was "surprised" when revival accompanied his preaching at Northampton in the eighteenth century, Charles G. Finney was not surprised that the correct use of "means" would produce conversion and renewal wherever he preached. This emphasis on personal experience found a home in some Congregational and Presbyterian churches, but it grew and flourished more successfully in the newer Baptist and Methodist churches.

Recent scholarship has emphasized the balance in Finney between the personal and social dimensions of faith. A mark of a renewed evangelicalism in our time is a rediscovery of Finney as a model for holding revivalism and social reform together. But Finney's followers did not always maintain this balance. Even later publications of Finney's works deliberately eliminated references to social reform so that the picture of Finney current in the early twentieth century was of a revivalism concerned almost exclusively with individual conversion.

Dwight L. Moody was the best-known successor to Finney. But the core of his message accentuated the focus on personal experience. A product of the city, Moody was aware of some of the problems of urban America, but he came to mistrust any theology directed at transforming society.

To be sure, personal experience was not meant to be private religion. It would be a caricature to say that conservative Protestantism and, later, fundamentalism had no social concern. The point is, any religion that focuses heavily on personal experience can become through time a religion that is basically a private matter.

The second dimension was the rapidly changing landscape of American religious traditions. In his famous *Plea for the West*, Lyman Beecher spoke prophetically of the great expansion that would occur in the Mississippi Valley and in the far West.

He feared the threat to democratic values of nineteenth-century Catholic authoritarianism, and was remarkably accurate in calculating the number of immigrants coming to America. His plea to audiences across the East called for harnessing the resources of the voluntary societies to settle this untamed land.

Neither the framers of the Constitution nor Beecher could have imagined the diversity that would develop in the nineteenth century. A mighty tide of immigrants made the Catholic Church the largest church in America. And in the latter part of the century various groups of Jews arrived from Europe. As in every land to which they came, their significance was always much greater than their numbers.

In addition to nurturing the religions of old Europe, American soil proved fruitful for distinctively American religions or variations of traditional religions. Communitarian movements combined old and new patterns of belief and behavior. The Mormons incorporated their own rendition of the New Israel motif in their uniquely American religion. The Disciples developed over time from sect to denomination. Christian Science arose in the midst of a new fascination with mind cure. Black churches, which combined African and American experiences, are unique in their appropriation of Christianity. Although sometimes mistakenly labeled fundamentalist, black churches more than white churches sought a balance between individual experience and concern for community and society. All of these religions shared a common desire for space for the development of their unique spirituality.

What this adds up to is a burgeoning pluralism. Until the end of the century there was remarkable consensus among the main bodies of Protestants, but the proliferation of churches, sects, and new religions spelled the ultimate doom of consensus.

The third dimension was individualism. Alexis de Toqueville, during his travels to America in the 1830s, was at once impressed and concerned with this phenomenon. Noting that "individualism" was a new word that best described this new nation, he wondered aloud about the trajectory of this individualism into the twentieth century. As he saw it, the Puritan vision of community was in tension with the Enlightenment emphasis on individualism. (Locke and various thinkers of the Enlightenment were the foundation of much of the conversation at the Constitutional convention about the "the rights of man.")

Toqueville suggested that three institutions—the family, politics, and religion—if they continued strong, would modify the tendency in America toward individualism. He believed it was the family's function to prepare or socialize people for their role in society. He was impressed by the participatory style of democracy, symbolized in the New England town meeting. Toqueville was also impressed by the churches' concern for society, and commented that the largest denominations functioned almost as political parties.

Robert N. Bellah and his colleagues, in *Habits of the Heart,* believe that each of these three institutions has lost or is losing its modifying role on individualism.[4] Families no longer see their role as preparing children for responsible service to society, but as preserves to perpetuate private values. Americans have lost the confidence that they can make a difference in the political process. Some of the harshest criticism is leveled at religion. American religion, from traditional churches to small sects and cults, has turned inward. Ministers have become therapists. Teachers of theology are writing for each other in specialized disciplines rather than constructing theologies and ethics for the good of society.

Some of the framers of the Constitution delighted in the diversity of religious denominations and sects in the colonies because they believed this very diversity was a chief ally in blocking establishment. Correct in this assessment, none of the framers could have envisioned the pluralistic society that is modern America. Cultural and religious individualism grew apace with pluralism, each reinforcing the other. In this kind of

4. Robert N. Bellah et al., *Habits of the Heart: Individualism and Commitment in American Life* (New York: Harper & Row, 1985).

culture religion has become more of a conforming than a transforming institution. Those churches and religious movements that flourish are the ones that adopt individualistic patterns.

III

For more than one hundred years after the final disestablishment occurred in Massachusetts, the First Amendment receded from the view of most Americans. This is not to say that Catholic immigrants were not concerned about what they believed to be a Protestant culture as represented in the developing public school system of the nineteenth century. Or that Jewish immigrants were not concerned about anti-Semitism in this so-called Christian country. But it is only within the last forty years, beginning with the Supreme Court case *Everson* v. *Board of Education* (1947), that the First Amendment has resurfaced through a whole series of cases argued before the courts, many reaching the Supreme Court. In our own day debates about prayer in public schools, creationism, religious celebrations, aid to private schools, and other issues have caused us to look again at the First Amendment.

The cumulative result of court decisions has been to protect the role of religion insofar as it is a personal or private matter, but to reduce the role of religion in society. It has been my experience that international students are much more aware of the private nature of American religion than are most Americans, with the exception of those who have been exposed to the revolutionary or reform possibilities of religion. Americans who have experienced life in, for example, Central America, often are greatly frustrated in acting, much less talking, about the role of religion in society upon their return to the United States.

At this point, I want to make some observations about how the trajectory toward private religion is alive and well today.

First, in a nation where people feel cut off from the sources of power, exemplified by cynicism about political participation, two entities—the local school system and the local church—

benefit from great participation. But they are experiencing increasing conflict. These two entities represent both hope and frustration—hope because of a high degree of concerned participation, and frustration, because more than ever before it is open season on school and church leaders. The criteria for evaluation and judgment often are not educational or theological. Both institutions are becoming politicized. There are unreal expectations for both school and church. Teachers are harassed by parents concerned about Billy or Susie's progress. Ministers are being questioned and challenged.

Expectations for both school and church are quite individualistic. Church information surveys show that members do not place a high priority on their church's involvement in social justice issues or ecumenical relations, both of which stem from an understanding of the importance of community. The pressure in schools on teachers is often not about preparation for responsible participation in society but about how an individual can get ahead in marching toward individual goals.

A second observation is that those churches that are flourishing at the end of this century are increasingly ones that are individualistic in both theology and government. The emphasis is on the benefits of church membership for the individual rather than the members' responsibility to society. The church growth movement, which offers itself as a new way to do evangelism, is based on a sociology that says that the way to grow is to stress homogeneity and to shun heterogeneity. Utilizing management techniques, seminars are offered wherein local church leaders learn how to eschew conflict and promote a congregation that its critics say looks more like a club than a church.

The churches that are growing are also individualistic in church government. At his seminars for church leaders, Robert Schuller has been saying recently that in the next century congregations that grow will shun associations with denominations. People do not want to come to Old First Methodist or First Presbyterian; rather, they will be coining new names—the Church of the Bright Morning Star—anything but names that conjure up denominational and thus big government images.

Ronald Reagan's criticism of big government is echoed across America by criticism of big denominations. While commentators have been aware of the appeal of theologically conservative churches, they have not given enough credit to the role the congregational form of government plays in that appeal. The churches that are growing may stress the Bible or the gifts of the Spirit, but they are also invariably congregational in form of government. Conversely, the mainline churches that are becoming oldline churches most often have more complex connectional rather than congregational forms of government.

But what about the public activity of Jerry Falwell and others of "the new right" who, against the grain of their tradition, have been mobilizing their constituencies for aggressive involvement with social issues in society? The important point is, which issues? Their focus is almost exclusively on issues of purity—pornography, homosexuality, abortion—which are seen as affecting the welfare of individuals and the sanctity of the family. They have not been involved with justice issues—poverty, racism, sexism, and war and peace.

These conservative churches are involved in the litigation on the First Amendment for a number of reasons. They want to preserve what they call the "Christian origins" of the nation. They believe that the country, and particularly the public education system, is becoming secular or is infected by what they label "secular humanism." People such as Jerry Falwell have moved from an apolitical posture to one where all the resources of modern corporate America—from lobbying to computers—are marshalled in the name of religious freedom.

On the other hand, the theologies of the so-called liberal churches have arisen from a more corporate understanding of faith, which translates into a vigorous social ethic. Often neglecting concern for purity issues such as pornography, they focus on issues of justice and peace.

The mainline churches have been in a quandary about First Amendment cases, which most often they have not acknowledged. That is, there has been a split between the leadership and the membership. For example, on the issue of prayer in public schools the leadership has sided with the courts, arguing that state approved brief prayer is not a viable solution and interferes with the rights of others. The membership sees prayer in public schools as a basic right in line with the Christian origins of the nation. They see secular humanism as the opponent and cannot understand why the leadership appears to be caving in in the name of tolerance. The conflict between leadership and membership over the issue of prayer in public schools reveals a deeper conflict over the understanding of the role of religion in society.

In conclusion, I believe it is possible to see a growing movement across religious communities that is alarmed by the tendency to discourage the historically vital role of religion in America. Both conservatives and liberals are frustrated. One result of this frustration is interest in the pattern of court decisions that many believe are prohibiting rather than protecting religious activity.

At the heart of the frustration is the conviction that moral values must be taught more effectively. Even though there has been a growing awareness of this problem in the religious communities, until now these communities have been unable to act together. Historic fears of a Protestant America and worries about a powerful Catholic Church are still heard wherever people gather to discuss these issues. More recently, mainstream Protestantism, Catholicism, and Judaism have been fearful of the fundamentalist religious right, and conservative Christians (including Catholics) express their fears of secular humanism.

Until now these fragmentations and fears have hampered united action. But there are signs that the seriousness of the problems may be just the catalyst needed for renewed dialogue leading to action. After a day at a Constitutional bicentennial convocation, Jewish, Catholic, and Protestant leaders agreed that the problem of the absence of values in our society was so great that the problem of how people of diverse traditions could agree on values was workable. A recurring theme that allowed the gathering to come to this conclusion was the recognition that religion was being reduced to purely personal experience. To accept this definition of religion was to give up the communal dimension central in each of these religious traditions.

What I found hopeful in so many of the lectures and discussions about the Constitution and the Bill of Rights was the vital discussion of the past, present, and future shape of religion in America. As I listened and participated I became much more aware of what I have called here the trajectory toward private religion. This trajectory is a direct, if often unintended, result of the acts of disestablishment. It is not helpful to bemoan what transpired, but it is instructive to reflect upon both the Puritan and Enlightenment traditions that underlie the origins of our nation. We need to become informed about the philosophies that have been guiding court decisions in the last four decades. The bicentennial of the Bill of Rights can then become the occasion to talk together about hopes for the shape of religion in the coming century.

Why It Took 150 Years for Supreme Court Church-State Cases to Escalate

Robert T. Handy

I

In 1955 Will Herberg, later to become a professor at Drew University, published a book with the title *Protestant-Catholic-Jew*. Many persons were startled and surprised by the work, and became aware of the meaning and significance of the pluriformity of American religion as if it were something recent. It seemed to be news to many people when he declared that "Protestantism today no longer regards itself either as a religious movement sweeping the continent or as a national church representing the religious life of the people; Protestantism understands itself today primarily as one of the three religious communities in which twentieth-century America has come to be divided."[1] That sweeping generalization was actually an oversimplification, for there were not three but a number of "religious communities,"

---

1. *Protestant-Catholic-Jew: An Essay in American Religious Sociology* (Garden City, N.Y.: Doubleday, 1955), pp. 139-40. On Herberg, see Harry J. Ausmus, *Will Herberg: From Right to Right* (Chapel Hill: Univ. of North Carolina Press, 1987).

as America had become a Catholic-Jewish-Eastern Orthodox-Protestant-Pentecostalist-Mormon-New Thought-Humanist nation, to list only some of the major options. The pluralistic patterns in fact had had a long history on the North American scene. Three hundred years ago Thomas Dongan, the governor of New York, reported that:

> New York has, first, a Chaplain belonging to the Fort, of the Church of England; secondly, a Dutch Calvinist; thirdly, a French Calvinist; fourthly, a Dutch Lutheran. Here bee not many of the Church of England, few Roman Catholicks; abundance of Quaker preachers, men and Women especially; Singing Quakers; Ranting Quakers; Sabbatarians; Anti-Sabbatarians; some Anabaptists; some Jews: in short, of all sorts of opinions there are some, and the most part of none at all.[2]

Though the religious situation in New York was then more pluralistic than that of most other towns of the time, nevertheless similar patterns were soon spreading in other parts of the land. Why did Herberg's book, not written until the middle of the twentieth century, come as such a surprise to so many?

To put the question another way: it was two centuries ago that the American Constitution was prepared with its provision in Article Six that "no religious Test shall ever be required as a qualification to any Office or public Trust under the United States." Before half a decade had passed, the First Amendment was prepared and ratified, the opening two clauses reading that "Congress shall make no law respecting an establishment of religion, or prohibiting the free exercise thereof. . . ." Yet with very few exceptions it was not until the 1940s, a century and a half later, that the flood of church-state cases before the Supreme Court crowded its dockets, a situation which continues unabated to the present. Why the sudden upsurge of litigation appealing to the religion clauses of the First Amendment a century and a half after they had been ratified?

---

2. As quoted by E. T. Corwin, *A History of the Reformed Church, Dutch* (New York, 1895), pp. 87-88.

II

The effort to provide historical answers to those two questions can well begin with a brief description of the religious situation of the 1780s, when the Constitution and its first ten amendments were prepared. Rough estimates of the relative size of the eleven largest denominations in the new nation, based on what we know of the number of congregations belonging to each, point to the following picture: the Congregationalists had more than 700 congregations, while the Presbyterians, Episcopalians, and Baptists held between 400 and 500 each. Then there were seven bodies varying in size from some 250 to about 60 congregations: Lutheran, German Reformed, Quaker, Dutch Reformed, Moravian, Mennonite, and Roman Catholic. The first ten in size were Protestant; the eleventh, claiming the allegiance of about 1 percent of the population, was generally regarded by the majority as a despised sect. Thus the actual religiously pluralistic situation was minimized by the claim that it was the Protestant churches, despite their theological differences, that dominated the religious life of the nation, and the opinion that this was and was to remain overwhelmingly a Protestant nation became deeply embedded.[3]

This view persisted through the nineteenth century despite some dramatic developments. In 1783 the president of Yale, Ezra Stiles, predicted in a sermon that three denominations—Congregational, Episcopal, Presbyterian—would tower over all the others and set the religious complexion of the young nation for the foreseeable future.[4] But how differently things turned out by the mid-nineteenth century, when the three churches he cited had fallen to fourth, seventh, and ninth places numerically, and three he would not have thought of mentioning in 1783 were the

3. Estimates drawn from Edwin S. Gaustad, *Historical Atlas of Religion in America* (New York, 1962), pp. 136, 158-61, 166; see also Willard L. Sperry, *Religion in America* (New York, 1946), p. 282.
4. "The United States Elevated to Glory and Honor," in *The Pulpit of the American Revolution,* ed. John W. Thornton, 2d ed. (Boston, 1876), pp. 467-72.

numerical giants: Roman Catholic, Methodist, and Baptist! He had no inkling that the small Catholic body would be so favored by trends in immigration, especially from Ireland and Germany, that it would become the largest single denomination in the United States by 1850. The Methodists had not even been founded as an independent church when he offered his prophecy, and though the Baptists were already probably the third largest group then, the prestigious president of Yale would have trouble seeing them as other than a lower-class sect. The latter two denominations had both participated fully in the waves of revivalistic fervor of the Second Great Awakening, and quickly surged numerically beyond such churches as the Congregational and the Presbyterian, which used the methods of mass revivalism with greater caution.

Though the barriers between the various Protestant churches remained high, and though there were many controversies and some dramatic schisms, they learned to work together to win America for Protestantism and to forestall what they saw as the Catholic menace through the pattern of the voluntary societies. Christians of differing backgrounds could join as individuals various societies for such causes as evangelism, home and foreign missions, common school and church college education, the publication of tracts and Bibles, and the reform of society. A central aim of what has been styled this "benevolent empire" of societies that came to be guided to a considerable extent by interlocking directorates was to make the United States a fully "Christian" nation as they defined it. They intended to undertake this work of evangelism and reform by persuasion only, thus professing to maintain religious freedom and the separation of church and state while striving to win everyone they could to their point of view. In politics they usually professed to be nonpartisan; it was unusual for one of them to call openly for a Christian party in politics, as Ezra Stiles Ely did in 1827 when he insisted that "every ruler *should be* an avowed and sincere friend of Christianity." Then, remembering the Constitution and the First Amendment, he added, "let Church and State be for ever distinct: but, still, let the doctrines and precepts of Christ govern all men, in all their relations and employments."[5] It was also not very often that a leader in the movement let show the implicit coerciveness behind the rhetoric of persuasion, as Charles G. Finney did ten years later. This great practitioner and theologian of revival was, like so many of his time, also a reformer with special interest in the temperance crusade as he used his oratorical skill to persuade his vast audiences to give up drink. When faced with strong opposition, he once observed that "multitudes will never yield, until the friends of God and man can form a public sentiment so strong as to crush the character of every man who will not give it up."[6]

More typically, the representatives of the quest for a Christian America argued that their voluntary approach would be unitive and not divisive and would not infringe on religious freedom. One of the prominent voices of the time, scholar and editor Bela Bates Edwards, once declared: "Perfect religious liberty does not imply that the government of the country is not a Christian government. . . . Most, if not all of our constitutions of government proceed on the basis of the truth of the Christian religion." He was convinced "that this real, though indirect, connection between the State and Christianity" was steadily gaining. He was also able to argue "that entire religious freedom does not involve the multiplication of religious sects, to a much greater degree, at least, than exists in some of those countries where religious freedom is but partially, or not at all, enjoyed." He reported that there was as great, or nearly as great, a number of religious groups in England and Scotland with their established churches as there were in America. He admitted that there were thirty or forty sects nominally in the United States, "but six or eight embrace the whole substantially."[7] Here one sees the painting of a picture of a kind of Protestant unity, one

5. From *The Duty of Christian Freemen to Elect Christian Rulers* (Philadelphia, 1828), as cited in *Church and State in American History: The Burden of Religious Pluralism*, ed. John Wilson and Donald L. Drakeman, 2d ed. (Boston, 1987), p. 96.

6. *Lectures to Professing Christians* (New York, 1837), p. 90.

7. *Writings of Professor B. B. Edwards* (Boston, 1853), 1:489-90.

that was still influential into the twentieth century and makes more intelligible the reaction to Herberg's famous book.

Edwards spoke as did his partners about Christianity, but clearly he meant Protestant Christianity, regarding with distaste and suspicion the remarkable growth of Roman Catholic Christianity. For him and for many others Catholicism was an alien in Protestant America, and as a "foreign" church it was a threat to their liberties. They brushed aside the protestations of the first American Catholic bishop, John Carroll, who many times spoke of "his earnest regard to preserve inviolate forever in our new empire the great principle of religious freedom."[8] Such views were reaffirmed many times by Catholic leaders, but were rarely taken seriously by Protestants. When a leading Protestant theologian, Horace Bushnell, prophesied that their crusade would soon mean that "the bands of a complete Christian commonwealth are seen to span the continent," he meant a Protestant commonwealth, for the title of the tract in which that appeared was *Barbarism the First Danger,* and readers of his essay knew that the second danger was "Romanism."[9] There were minorities all too ready to match such expressions with action, as in the burning of a convent in Massachusetts in the 1830s and churches in Pennsylvania in the following decade.

The Protestant denominations found an important point of unity in their conspicuous support for the public schools— the common schools, as they were then generally known. In his famous study of America, Alexis de Tocqueville observed that though the sects differed in modes of worship they "preached the same moral law in the name of God."[10] Thus the Protestant churches could work together on behalf of public education as a benefit to all and an instrument of morality in their striving for a fully Christian commonwealth. "It is difficult today," writes a twentieth-century scholar of education, "to recapture the tone

8. As quoted by Peter Guilday, *The Life and Times of John Carroll* (New York, 1922), 1:368.

9. *Barbarism the First Danger: A Discourse for Home Missions* (New York: 1847), quotation on p. 32.

10. *Democracy in America,* Bradley edition (New York, 1945), 1:103.

of thought and feeling of those who saw the common school as an integral part of their crusade to create the Kingdom of God across the land."[11] By mid-century, they had found means to advance their many cases in a way they found consistent with the nation's basic constitutional documents.

III

The tensions aroused by the slavery issue and the Civil War sidetracked the quest for a "Christian" America, but it was soon renewed. One of the clearest illustrations of its continuation was Grant's "peace policy" in Indian affairs, put into effect in 1869. This allowed the churches to control the government agents on Indian reservations and greatly expanded the program of federal aid to missions and schools. Only seven of the seventy-three agencies were in the hands of Catholics, despite the extent of their work on the reservations. As one recent scholar, Robert H. Keller, Jr., has summarized the way the peace policy worked, it "replaced the spoils system with church patronage, provided federal support for sectarian missions and worship, violated the constitutional ban against religious tests for public office, and . . . denied religious liberty as guaranteed by the First Amendment." He concluded that it "can be viewed equally as the culmination of the idea of a Christian Commonwealth and as a flagrant violation of the First Amendment, but the second probability simply did not occur to many people in the 1870s."[12] The policy was terminated in 1882, but some of its arrangements were continued in the provision for contract schools under church auspices. Small wonder that the famous British observer of American life Lord James Bryce could say in 1888 that "Christianity is understood to be, though not the legally estab-

11. "The Kingdom of God and the Common School," *Harvard Educational Review* 36 (1966): 455.

12. *American Protestantism and United States Indian Policy, 1869–82* (Lincoln, Neb., 1983), pp. 176, 213.

lished religion, yet the national religion."[13] The leaders of American Protestantism also felt themselves to be a part of a world movement destined to win; as one theologian put the matter in 1890, "the future of the world seems to be in the hands of the three great Protestant powers—England, Germany, and the United States. The old promise is being fulfilled; the followers of the true God are inheriting the world."[14] It sounds strange to our ears now to read in a Supreme Court decision an *obiter dictum* about how Christian the nation was. The words were written by Associate Justice David J. Brewer, but no dissent was recorded, so the prestige of the Court stood behind the opinion. The passage called attention to the various state constitutions which provided "organic utterances" which "speak the voice of the entire people" that the Christian religion was part of the common law, and summarized with a list of particulars:

> If we pass beyond these matters to a view of American life as expressed by its laws, its business, its customs, and its society, we find everywhere a recognition of the same truth. Among other matters note the following: The form of oath universally prevailing, concluding with an appeal to the Almighty; the custom of opening sessions of all deliberative bodies and most conventions with prayer; the prefatory words of all wills, "In the name of God, amen"; the laws respecting the observance of the Sabbath, with the general cessation of all secular business, and the closing of courts, legislatures, and other similar public assemblies on that day; the churches and church organizations which abound in every city, town, and hamlet; the multitude of charitable organizations existing everywhere under Christian auspices; the gigantic missionary associations, with general support, and aiming to establish Christian missions in every quarter of the globe. These, and many other matters which might be noticed, add a volume of unofficial declarations to the mass of organic utterances that this is a Christian nation.[15]

13. *The American Commonwealth* (London, 1888), 3:474.
14. Lewis French Stearns, *The Evidence of Christian Experience* (New York, 1890), p. 366.
15. As quoted by Anson Phelps Stokes, *Church and State in the United States* (New York, 1950), 3:571-72. Brewer later wrote *The United States a Christian Nation* (Philadelphia, 1905).

Looking back on those years, historian Sidney Mead observed that "under the system of official separation of church and state the denominations eventually found themselves as completely identified with nationalism and their country's political and economic systems as had ever been known in Christendom."[16]

IV

All during the last half of the nineteenth and into the twentieth century, the population was rapidly increasing, from 17 million in 1850 to more than four times that number in 1900, 76 million, and then doubling to 151 million in 1950. As streams of immigrants brought mounting numbers from central, southern, and eastern Europe the Catholic, Eastern Orthodox, and Jewish elements in the nation increased markedly. The number of Protestant denominations also multiplied for a variety of reasons, including immigration, schisms over slavery and race, the burgeoning of the black denominations, the increase of New Thought and other harmonial groups, and the impact of the Holiness and Pentecostal movements. All this meant a dramatic increase in the pluriformity of religion in America, and some challenges to the assumptions of the older, well-entrenched churches. The rapidly growing giant among churches, the Roman Catholic, by the turn of the century far larger than its nearest numerical rivals, especially objected to the concept of a Christian America that left it out. The religious overtones of the supposedly nonsectarian but actually predominantly Protestant public schools were especially troubling to the Catholics. In 1884 the hierarchy launched a determined drive to expand the parochial school system wherever there was a Catholic parish. This led to some ugly reactions, and to the formation of the American Protective Association three years later, for to many Protestants and some others the concern that every Catholic child have an opportunity for

16. *The Lively Experiment: The Shaping of Christianity in America* (New York, 1963), p. 157.

parochial school education appeared as an attack on the common schools.[17] A casualty of the increased Catholic-Protestant tension was the end of the last vestige of the Grant peace policy, the contract schools. Francis Paul Prucha concluded that "the close ties between the churches and the government in Indian matters were finally cut by the sharp knife of intolerance" as Protestants chose to withdraw from the arrangement, "preferring to lose their own meager benefits than to see the Catholics profit."[18] Keller observed that "not until American Catholicism began to grow in size did 'strict separation' become a constitutional doctrine."[19]

At the dawn of the new century, however, Protestant leaders were confident about the future. They faced the new century with a burst of enthusiasm, energy, and hope, buoyed up and given a sense of unity by an expectation of the coming kingdom of God, and confident that their dream of a Christian America would soon be fulfilled. When the Federal Council of Churches was formed in 1908 the delegates from more than thirty Protestant denominations were welcomed by a prominent Presbyterian, William H. Roberts, who delared that the new organization would seek "the thorough Christianization of our country" and that it would stand for "speedy Christian advance toward World Conquest."[20] The passage of the Eighteenth Amendment on prohibition, backed by much of Protestant America, seemed to be a step along the way, and the defeat of a Catholic candidate for president in 1928 made the Protestant future seem secure.

17. See Lloyd P. Jorgenson, *The State and the Non-Public School, 1825–1925* (Columbia, Mo., 1987), and Donald L. Kinzer, *An Episode in Anti-Catholicism: The American Protective Association* (Seattle, 1964).

18. *American Indian Policy in Crisis: Christian Reformers and the Indian, 1865–1900* (Norman, Okla., 1976), pp. 56, 318.

19. *American Protestantism and United States Indian Policy,* p. 214.

20. "Welcome to the Federal Council: Its Character, Purpose, and Spirit Outlined," in *Federal Council of the Churches of Christ in America: Report of the First Meeting,* ed. Elias B. Sanford (New York, 1909), p. 323.

V

In a tangled series of events, however, the bubble of Protestant confidence was pricked in the 1920s, and the ability of its leaders to speak as though they had a working religious majority decreased as the century wore on. The pervasive transformations wrought in society by what had happened during World War I became increasingly clear and made many of the patterns of the years just preceding its impact seem remote. As Barbara Tuchman has so powerfully put it, "The Great War of 1914-18 lies like a band of scorched earth dividing that time from ours."[21] On the domestic scene the war played some role in deepening rifts between theological parties in the Protestant world when the bitter fundamentalist/modernist controversy was at its peak in 1925. The growing secularization in the culture was especially perplexing for churches that had been so confident of their cultural role. One might try to dismiss journalist H. L. Mencken's comment that "Protestantism in this great Christian realm is down with a wasting disease"[22] as the gibe of an unfriendly critic, but the observation of Episcopal bishop Charles Fiske was as blunt when he described "a sad disintegration of American Protestantism."[23] What happened in the early depression years was aptly summarized by historian Theodore H. White: "This American Protestant culture dominated politics until 1932—when all of it broke down in the marketplace. . . ."[24] What I have elsewhere called "the second disestablishment" of American Protestantism—this time the disestablishment of the idea and practice of a voluntary Christendom—was clearly under way.[25] A man who for many decades was a wise and perceptive church leader, Samuel McCrea Cavert, exclaimed in 1937 that "we can no longer discuss the relation of Church and State, even in America, on the basis of

21. *The Proud Tower* (New York, 1966), p. xiii.
22. *American Mercury* 4 (1925): 286.
23. *Confessions of a Troubled Parson* (New York, 1928), p. 191.
24. *In Search of History* (New York, 1978), p. 626.
25. *A Christian America: Protestant Hopes and Historical Realities,* 2d ed. (New York, 1984), chap. 7.

the old assumptions which have held the field down to our own day."[26] Though many only later became aware of it, during the depression the "Protestant era" in American history came to a close. For some this seemed to mean the loss of religion itself, for others it meant the freeing of religion from old alliances that were outdated and had become dysfunctional. Perceptions of the realities of religious life only slowly dawned on many people as awareness of the actual changes, especially the growing pluriformity of religious institutions, spread unevenly. Much depended on what part of the country one lived in, and how much one's own religious horizon revolved around a given tradition. In part because of the continuing assumption that this was a Christian nation—as late as 1931 the Supreme Court observed that "we are a Christian people"[27]—it only slowly became widely recognized that the spectrum of denominations was steadily widening as various new groups such as (for example) the Jehovah's Witnesses enlarged their circle of followers, as Judaism had grown into a major religious movement with its own extensive network of divisions and institutions, as the Latter-day Saints became one of the larger churches, and as the number of groups related to other world religions was increasing.

VI

This article began with two questions: Why did Herberg's book of 1955 come as such a surprise as it dramatized American religious pluralism, and why did the number of Supreme Court church-state cases mushroom so dramatically after 1940? To comment in chronological order, by the latter date various court cases were dramatizing a rapidly changing religious situation. At local levels, for example, clashes arose as familiar laws and

26. "Points of Tension between Church and State in America Today," in *Church and State in the Modern World,* ed. Henry P. Van Dusen et al. (New York, 1937), p. 191.

27. *United States* v. *Macintosh,* 283 U.S. 625 (1931).

customs that reflected the older Protestant era were challenged. An important constitutional development opened the way for the Court to deal with such matters. The Fourteenth Amendment (1868) had included the clause "No State shall make or enforce any law which shall abridge the privileges or immunities of citizens of the United States." In a case in 1940, *Cantwell* v. *Connecticut,* the Court unanimously upheld the right of Jehovah's Witnesses to propagate their faith publicly and engage in door-to-door solicitation without a permit. In so doing, the Supreme Court specifically incorporated the free exercise clause of the First Amendment into the Fourteenth, thereby making it applicable to the states.[28] Then, seven years later in *Everson* v. *Board of Education,* a New Jersey school bus case, in a close decision (5-4) the Court found that parents of parochial as well as public school children should be reimbursed for fares spent in getting children to school, and in so doing also incorporated the Establishment Clause into the First Amendment.[29] Thus, a century and a half after the First Amendment had been ratified, its clauses on religion were finally applied to the states. During the nineteenth century what I have called voluntary Christendom as promoted by general agreements among most of the leading Protestant denominations seemed to push opposing movements, including a growing and massive Catholicism, into "minority" status, until the growing strengths of many minorities, coupled with the slow recognition that the situation was indeed changing, led to the new situation that emerged in the 1940s.

Herberg's *Protestant-Catholic-Jew* did not discuss the court cases, but was an effort at analysis of the American religious situation in the 1950s in the midst of an upturn in religious vitality. Among other things, the analysis highlighted the significance of immigration and its contributions to the pluralization of religion in America. Two of the chapters had as primary titles "From the Land of Immigrants to the Triple Melting Pot," and

28. 310 U.S. 296 (1940).
29. 330 U.S. 1 (1947).

five others profiled, compared, and contrasted the three main "communities" of the book's title. It proved to be a dramatic though oversimplified way of emphasizing what had happened to American religious life, and led to a new awareness among many persons of the twentieth-century significance of the religious pluriformity that had long been a reality.

To conclude: the term *church and state* was never really accurate for the American scene, at least not since the colonial legal establishments of Congregationalism in three New England states and Anglicanism in five southern states (and partly in New York) had disappeared. But the fact that in its place we have a growing network of religious movements and associations on the one hand and an expanding system of governmental agencies at local, state, and national levels on the other was to a large measure obscured through the nineteenth century by the Protestant effort to make America a Christian nation as it defined it—a Christendom to be won by voluntary means. As a result of such forces as vast immigration, the freeing of black people to go their own way religiously, and the founding of many new movements, the older pattern was finally largely pushed aside and new ways of dealing with tensions between denominations and their relationships with governmental agencies had to be found. One important way of doing this was to appeal to the religion clauses of the First Amendment, and so we moved into the period in which we now are, one marked by considerable controversy and litigation. I began with two questions and have tried to answer them, but find myself struggling with another one with which I close: can we find a way to balance the approach to the so-called church-state problem through constitutional and legal issues with a more general awareness for the concerns and commitments of others about matters of religion, and allow ourselves to see more fully that we are not dealing with abstractions labeled church and state but with a vast double network of religious associations of many kinds and of governmental agencies of many types?

PART III:
AN UNSETTLED ARENA

The Establishment Clause:
The Never-Ending Conflict

Leo Pfeffer

I. Introduction

According to Lewis Carroll's report, "When *I* use a word," said
Humpty Dumpty, "it means just what I choose it to mean—
neither more nor less." Translated into the constitutional law
language in relation to the First Amendment, the Establishment
Clause means just what the Supreme Court or a majority thereof
at any particular time wants it to mean, neither more nor less.

That's not to say that the Court does not try. In *Everson* v.
Board of Education,[1] upholding by 5-4 the state financing of bus
transportation to parochial schools, the Court ruled—and here
there was no dissent—that although the First Amendment reads
"*Congress* shall make no law respecting an establishment of religion" (my italics), this prohibition also applies to actions by the
states. How so? Well, the Fourteenth Amendment forbids states
from depriving "any person of life, liberty, or property, without
due process of law." Liberty, said the Court, means more than

---

1. *Everson* v. *Board of Education*, 330 U.S. 1 (1947).

physical restraint as in the case of a person charged with criminal action; it means as well the liberty of not being forced through taxation to support a religion in which one does not believe, and indeed even a religion in which one does believe.

This happened in 1947. A year later, in *McCollum* v. *Board of Education*,[2] the Court applied this interpretation of the Establishment Clause to hold unconstitutional an Illinois law that allowed teachers of religions—Protestant, Catholic, and Jewish—to come into public school classrooms and teach the principles and practices of their respective faiths to those pupils whose parents agreed.

This decision aroused considerable protest from Protestants (though not all Protestants), from Catholics (though not all Catholics), but, with rare exceptions, *not* from Jews, and of course not from persons who were later to be called "Secular Humanists." The Supreme Court, said the protesters, had misread the Establishment Clause in respect to both its meaning and its applicability to the states.

So persistent and vigorous were these protests that fifteen years after *McCollum* in *Abington Township School District* v. *Schempp*,[3] which invalidated public school prayer practices, the Court found it necessary to go out of its way in an effort to put an end to the controversy. In its written opinion, the Court said the following:

> While none of the parties have questioned these basic conclusions of the Court [relating to the meaning and applicability of the Establishment Clause], both of which have been long established, recognized and consistently reaffirmed, others continue to question their history, logic and efficacy. Such contentions in the light of the consistent interpretation of the cases of this Court, seem entirely untenable and of value only as academic exercises.

For better or for worse, the Court's hope proved futile. As will be seen in the course of this chapter, the assault upon what

---

2. *McCollum* v. *Board of Education*, 330 U.S. 203 (1948).
3. *Abington Township School District* v. *Schempp*, 374 U.S. 203 (1963).

has become known as the absolutist or strict separationist interpretation of the Establishment Clause is still alive, and is in fact
growing in intensity. The major attack comes from the so-called
accommodationists, who seek to return religious practices to the
public schools (e.g., former President Reagan and Senator Jesse
Helms of North Carolina), and/or promote use of tax-raised
funds to support parochial schools (e.g., spokesmen for the
Catholic Church and Orthodox Judaism). Moreover, two vigorous and persistent assailants have come on the scene recently:
fundamentalists, who demand the return of prayer and religious
instruction to the public schools and who find "Secular
Humanism" to be a religion and hence not allowable in the public schools, and those persons—fundamentalists or not—who
challenge the claims of so-called cultists to equal treatment with
accepted religions.

My purpose here is to examine each of these positions and
to consider their validity under the Establishment Clause.

II. The Absolutist Approach

Those defending strict separation recognize that realistically the
absolute separation of church and state is not possible; churches
will continue to be exempt from taxation, and presidents will add
"So help me God" when they take their oath of office. But what
does that prove? Does the reality that no person is immortal mean
that the medical and pharmaceutical professions should be
abolished? Realistic separationists recognize that the complete
separation of church and state cannot be achieved, but that is the
direction in which they would have government go. They maintain that those in Congress and in the states who drafted and
adopted the Establishment Clause were more akin to the absolutists than to those who call themselves accommodationists.

The evidence to support this conclusion antedates the
adoption of the First Amendment. The Constitution itself makes
no reference to the Deity, and the only reference it makes to religion is a negative one. The text of the Constitution ends with

the mandate: "no religious test shall ever be required as a qualification to any office or public trust under the United States."
There are no exceptions to this—not even in respect to outright
atheists—and it is difficult to explain it other than as a mandate
of absolute separation of religion and state.[4]

The preadoption history of the Establishment Clause leads
to the same conclusion. Justice Rutledge sets it forth in detail in
his dissenting opinion in the *Everson* case, as does Justice Black,
to a lesser extent, in his majority opinion.

These opinions and many other historic resources lead to
the conclusion, stated a century ago by the noted constitutional
advocate Jeremiah S. Black, that the

> manifest object of the men who framed the institution of this
> country, was to have a State without religion and a Church
> without politics—that is to say, they meant that one should never
> be used as an engine for the purposes of the other. . . . For that
> they built up a wall of complete partition between the two.[5]

The historic background of the Establishment (as well as
the Free Exercise) Clause reveals what would seem to be two dis-
parate sources: the deep religiosity, in large measure but by no
means exclusively, of the Baptists; and the deism of Thomas
Jefferson, James Madison, and Tom Paine, among others. (In
1776, Paine wrote in *Common Sense,* "As to religion, I hold it to be
the indispensable duty of government to protect all conscientious
protesters thereof, and I know of no other business government
has to do therewith.") Deism assumes a belief in a God who
created the world but who left to the people thereof its further
control and management.

Recognizing the evils of man acting like God or of man's
using government to help God out in managing the world, the
traditional religionists, such as disciples of Roger Williams, Isaac

---

4. For further consideration, see Leo Pfeffer, "The Deity in American Constitutional History," in *Religion and the State: Essays in Honor of Leo Pfeffer,* ed.
James Wood, Jr. (Waco, Tex.: Baylor Univ. Press, 1985), pp. 185-219.

5. Jeremiah S. Black, *Essays and Speeches,* (D. Appleton and Co., 1885),
p. 53.

Backus, and John Leland, joined with the deists in fashioning a system in which neither belief nor disbelief in God was to be a matter within the jurisdiction of human government. Both groups sought to secure a government that neither aided nor injured religion, and for this both the Establishment and Free Exercise Clauses of the First Amendment were adopted.[6]

The Supreme Court's interpretation of the Establishment Clause, voiced first in *Everson* and later in many other cases, forbade government aid to religion. In the more recent cases the Court worded the clause somewhat differently from the no-aid formula; it held violative of the clause governmental action if it lacked a secular purpose or if its principal or primary effect was either to advance or inhibit religion or if it entailed excessive governmental entanglement with religion.[7] The basic principle was not altered; in many cases the Court has invoked both the no-aid principle of *Everson* and the purpose-effect-entanglement criteria of later cases.

III. The Accommodationist Approach

There is, however, another side to this history. Protagonists of governmental aid to religious schools were quite pleased with the Court's ruling in the *Everson* case, but before long they recognized that its basic premise was not what they wanted. In the *McCollum* case, decided in the Court's next term, it used that premise to invalidate an Illinois law providing for the teaching of religion in the public schools.

In his argument before the Court in the latter case, the coun-

6. "Of the eleven states that ratified the First Amendment, nine (counting Maryland) adhered to the viewpoint that support of churches should be voluntary, that any government financial assistance to religion constituted an establishment of religion and violated its free exercise." Thomas J. Curry, *The First Freedoms: Church and State in America to the Passage of the First Amendment* (New York: Oxford Univ. Press, 1986), p. 220.

7. *Walz* v. *Tax Commission*, 397 U.S. 664 (1970); *Lemon* v. *Kurtzman*, 403 U.S. 602 (1971); *Committee for Public Education and Religious Liberty* v. *Nyquist*, 413 U.S. 756 (1973).

sel for the school board relied on the manuscript of a book that challenged the Court's interpretation of the Establishment Clause. In the book,[8] Professor James M. O'Neill termed "spurious" the so-called "great American principle of complete separation of church and state," and asserted that "there is no such great principle and there never has been." The purpose of the Establishment Clause, said O'Neill, was to forbid congressional action that sought to make one religion the established religion of the nation, or to prefer one or more religions over others. It was not the intent of those who drafted and adopted the First Amendment to bar the general support of religion in government, and the clause therefore does not prohibit the nonpreferential expenditure for religious purposes of funds raised by general taxation.

This understanding of the clause was shared by Professor Edward S. Corwin, a noted constitutional scholar, and other authorities. Later advocates of the principle included Robert C. Antieau, A. Downey, and E. Roberts, authors of *Freedom From Federal Establishment* (1964). Another was Michael Malbin, who in his book, *Religion and Politics,* said:

> Had the framers prohibited "*the* establishment of religion," which would have emphasized the generic word "religion," there might have been some reason for thinking they wanted to prohibit all official preferences of religion over irreligion. But by choosing "an establishment" over "the establishment," they were showing that they wanted to prohibit only those official activities that tended to promote the interests of one or another particular sect.

A more recent advocate of this position is Professor Robert L. Cord, author of *Separation of Church and State: Historical Fact and Current Fiction* (1982). This book has received considerable praise and endorsement from, among others, New York Senator Daniel Patrick Moynihan and Professor Charles E. Rice of Notre Dame Law School and co-editor-in-chief of *The American Journal of Jurisprudence.* Professor Rice's endorsement on the back cover of the book reads:

8. James M. O'Neill, *Religion and Education Under the Constitution* (Harper and Brothers, 1949).

This compelling study demonstrates that the prevailing view of the religion clauses of the First Amendment is not only unwise but fictional. If heeded by the Supreme Court, Professor Cord's analysis will profoundly alter our constitutional future.

In his dissenting opinion in the 1985 case of *Wallace* v. *Jaffree*,[9] Justice (later Chief Justice) Rehnquist accepted the views of these and other authorities. However, the majority of the Court ruled that an Alabama statute requiring elementary school teachers to begin each day with a one-minute period of silent prayer violated the Establishment Clause.

To Justice Rehnquist the Court has been in error ever since it adopted the *Everson* no-aid and the later purpose-effect-entanglement tests of the Establishment Clause. It was not, he said, the intent of those who wrote and approved the Establishment Clause that the government be absolutely neutral between religion and irreligion. The evil the clause sought to avoid was the establishment of a national church or an "assertion by the Federal Government of a preference for one religious denominational sect over others," but it was definitely not intended to forbid government aid if it was offered to all religions evenhandedly. Since a moment of silent prayer obviously fulfilled the requirement of nonpreference, it was clearly constitutional, as were all the relevant rulings since the *Everson* decision was handed down.

Justice Rehnquist cited the books of O'Neill, Cord, and Antineau, Downey, and Roberts, which place considerable reliance upon the nineteenth-century writings of Thomas Cooley and Joseph Story. Story, he noted, was a member of the Supreme Court from 1811 to 1845 and during much of that time was also a professor at Harvard Law School. To support his position, Justice Rehnquist quoted the following from Story's *Commentaries on the Constitution of the United States:*

> Probably at the time of the adoption of the Constitution, and of the [First] amendment to it now under consideration the general if not

9. *Wallace* v. *Jaffree*, 105 S. Ct. 2479, 2508 et. seq. (1985).

the universal sentiment in America was that Christianity ought to receive encouragement from the State so far as it was not incompatible with the private rights of conscience and the freedom of religious worship. An attempt to level all religions, and to make it a matter of state policy to hold all in utter indifference, would have created universal disapprobation, if not universal indignation. . . .

The real object of the amendment was not to countenance, much less to advance, Mahometanism, or Judaism, or infidelity, by prostrating Christianity; *but to exclude all rivalry among Christian sects,*[10] and to prevent any national ecclesiastical establishment which should give to a hierarchy the exclusive patronage of the national government. It thus cut off the means of religious persecution (the vice and pest of former ages), and of the subversion of the rights of conscience in matters of religion, which had been trampled upon almost from the days of the Apostles to the present age.

Justice Rehnquist, near the end of his opinion, summarized his position as follows:

The Framers intended the Establishment Clause to prohibit the designation of any church as a "national" one. The Clause was also designed to stop the Federal Government from asserting a preference for one religious denomination or sect over others. Given the "incorporation" of the establishment clause as against the States via the Fourteenth Amendment in *Everson,* States are prohibited as well from establishing a religion or discriminating between sects. As its history abundantly shows, however, nothing in the Establishment Clause requires government to be strictly neutral between religion and irreligion, nor does that Clause prohibit Congress or the States from pursuing legitimate secular ends through nondiscriminatory sectarian means.

It should be noted that, as the majority opinion in the *Wallace* case pointed out, the *amicus curiae* brief submitted by the United States solicitor general in support of the state's position argued that Alabama's moment-of-silence was merely an "accommodation" of the desire of many public school children to practice their religion by praying silently.

---

10. It is difficult to reconcile the italicized portion with the accommodationists' premise of equality among religions.

The government was apparently not ready to follow Justice Rehnquist in annulling all the relevant Supreme Court decisions since the *Everson* decision. It did, however, endorse the accommodationists' position that nothing in the language of the Establishment Clause or its history as it was understood by those who wrote or adopted it can be construed as barring non-preferential governmental accommodation to the needs of religious institutions and the pupils who attend them.

IV. The Fundamentalists' Claim

In recent years, particularly after Ronald Reagan became president, fundamentalists—who generally now prefer to call themselves evangelicals or born-again Christians—have become a significant political force in the United States. (The term *fundamentalists* and its synonyms are used here to designate Christians who believe in the literal truth of everything in the Bible, and particularly in the New Testament. Among Jews, their equivalents are called *hasidim*—plural for *hasid*—although, of course, to them the Bible is only the Old Testament.)

Fundamentalists' claim to tax exemption reached the Supreme Court in the early years of Reagan's presidency. In *Walz* v. *Tax Commission*[11] the Court had ruled in 1970 that the Establishment Clause was not violated by according real estate tax exemption in respect to houses of worship. Later, in the companion cases of *Bob Jones University* v. *United States* and *Goldsboro Christian Schools* v. *United States*,[12] the Court was called upon to determine whether two fundamentalist colleges could be denied tax exemption because of their policies in respect to the admission and retention of students who were not of the white race.

In both cases, school administrators sincerely believed that race mixing was against God's will and they contended that to

11. *Walz* v. *Tax Commission*, 397 U.S. 664 (1970).
12. *Bob Jones University* v. *United States*, and *Goldsboro Christian Schools* v. *United States*, 397 U.S. 574 (1983).

deny them tax exemption for complying with his will would violate the First Amendment's guarantee of the free exercise of religion. In the *Bob Jones* case counsel contended that it would also violate the Establishment Clause.

The Goldsboro school had been established to give "special emphasis on the Christian religion and the ethics revealed in Holy Scripture." Its founder believed that race is determined by descent from one of Noah's three sons, Ham (Orientals and blacks), Shem (Jews), and Japtheh (caucasians). School officials regarded cultural or biological race mixing as violating God's command, and accordingly they maintained a racially exclusionary admission policy.

The sponsors of Bob Jones University were more liberal in their admission policy, but they too were genuine in their belief that the Bible adjudged interracial dating and marriage to be sinful, and they forbade, under penalty of expulsion, the commission of either of those sins.

In 1971 the Supreme Court in *Coit* v. *Green*[13] had upheld the action of the Internal Revenue Service in refusing to accord tax-exempt status to a Mississippi private school that discriminated against blacks. On the basis of this decision, the IRS denied tax-exemption status to the Bob Jones and Goldsboro Christian schools. Howver, during the election campaign of 1980 Reagan promised the Bob Jones officials that he would restore their tax-exemption status because he agreed with them that denial of exemption violated the First Amendment. Accordingly, he directed the Department of Justice to reverse its position and to defend the schools' claim to exemption. The Supreme Court, with the exception of Justice Rehnquist, ruled that the IRS's initial position was correct and that the schools could not receive tax exemption notwithstanding their First Amendment claims under the Free Exercise Clause, and in the *Bob Jones* case the additional claim under the Establishment Clause.[14]

13. *Coit* v. *Green*, 404 U.S. 997 (1971), affirming *Green* v. *Connally*, 630 F. Supp. 1150.

14. *Bob Jones University* v. *United States*, and *Goldsboro Christian Schools* v. *United States*, 397 U.S. 574 (1983).

In respect to the former claim, the Court held that governmental interest in eradicating racial discrimination was compelling and outweighed the schools' claim to Free Exercise inasmuch as there were no less restrictive means to eradicate the racial discrimination. In respect to the Establishment Clause, which is our concern here, the Court rejected the Bob Jones' contention that the clause was violated because it preferred religions whose tenets do not require racial discrimination over those that believe racial intermixing to be forbidden by God. A regulation, the Court said, does not violate the Establishment Clause in that it happens by coincidence to harmonize with some or all religions. Moreover, as the Court of Appeals had noted, the uniform application of the rule avoids the necessity for a potentially entangling inquiry into whether a racially restrictive practice is the result of a sincere religious belief. (Admittedly, this last justification seems weak. Aside from the fact that in this case all parties conceded that the school was sincere in enforcing its exclusionary regulation, there is the more significant difficulty that ever since the Supreme Court's decision in the *Ballard* case[15] sincerity is a factual question to be determined by the trial judge or jury whenever it is relevant to the controversy before the court—but as suggested at the beginning of this chapter, also relevant is Humpty Dumpty's ruling that a word means what the judicial authority chooses it to mean.)

Another case involving the Establishment Clause, *Edwards* v. *Aguillard*, dealt with the teaching of evolution in public schools of Louisiana. The background to this case occurred in 1968 in the *Epperson* case,[16] where the Court had ruled unconstitutional under the Establishment Clause an Arkansas statute that made it unlawful for a teacher in any state-supported school or university "to teach the theory or doctrine that mankind ascended or descended from a lower order of animals," or "to adopt the use in any such institution a textbook that teaches [this] theory." Since that decision was handed down, and especially since Reagan be-

15. *United States* v. *Ballard*, 322 U.S. 78 (1944).
16. *Epperson* v. *Arkansas*, 393 U.S. 97 (1968).

came president, fundamentalists have sought means of annulling or weakening the ruling as far as possible.

Some have sought to call upon the Court to overrule itself and uphold a measure that would forbid the teaching of subjects that contradict the creation and the flood as related in the Book of Genesis. The more realistic of them recognized that such a resolution, though highly to be desired, was very much unlikely. What they agreed upon instead was a measure that appealed to the American sense of fairness. Although introduced in a number of states, the measure was enacted in Louisiana. It provided that if a school elected to teach "Evolution-science," defined as "the scientific evidence for evolution and inferences from those scientific evidences," it was required to accord equal time for the "Creation-science," defined as "the scientific evidence for creation and inferences from those scientific evidences," and *vice versa*. No school, however, was required to teach both "sciences," and one can hardly doubt that the protagonists of this measure would be most happy if the schools elected to choose the option of silence.

It should be noted that the legislators, on the advice of counsel, carefully avoided the use of such words as *God, the Bible,* or *the Book of Genesis.* Noteworthy too is the fact that among the plaintiffs seeking to have the law declared unconstitutional were seven nonfundamentalist clergymen of the Protestant, Catholic, and Jewish faiths. Moreover, among the many *amicus curiae* (friend-of-the-court) briefs supporting the plaintiffs' challenge to the statute was that of the National Council of Churches of Christ in the United States of America. The sum total of all this was that the Louisiana law reflected, on the whole, only fundamentalist concerns.

From this, it would seem obvious that the statute violated the Establishment Clause no less than did the Arkansas statute in the *Epperson* case. And this indeed is what the Supreme Court held. The plaintiffs had challenged the statute on all three parts of the purpose-effect-entanglement formula. The Court did not find it necessary to consider the effect-entanglement aspects of the Establishment Clause; the purpose barrier was adequate, since it was obvious that it was the purpose of the Louisiana legislature to advance the fundamentalists' religious belief in the Book of Genesis even though there was no reference to it in the statute.[17]

V. The "Religiosity" of Secular Humanism

Another recent arena in which champions of fundamentalism are manifesting their not insignificant power in affecting legislative and judicial law deals with the so-called Secular Humanism. I must admit that I am to some extent responsible for the entrance of that term into the arena of constitutional law. Here is how it came about.

In 1961 I argued the case of *Torcaso* v. *Watkins*[18] before the Supreme Court. It involved the denial by the State of Maryland of an atheist's application for a certificate to act as a notary public because of his refusal to comply with a statute requiring all state officials to declare a belief in the existence of God. In both my brief and my oral argument, I asserted, and the Court agreed, that the law violated the First Amendment's clause forbidding laws respecting an establishment of religion, and also its guarantee of freedom of belief (on the ground that freedom to believe encompasses freedom not to believe).

In my brief I stated further (unnecessarily) that not all religions were based on a belief in the existence of a personal God. "The First Amendment," I said, "protects the Buddhist, Ethical Culturist and other nontheists no less than it does the Protestant, Roman Catholic and Jew."

What came out of this was Footnote 11 of Justice Black's opinion for the Court. There he wrote: "Among religions in this country, however, which do not teach what would generally be considered belief in the existence of God are Buddhism, Taoism, Ethical Culture, Secular Humanism and others."

17. *Aguillard* v. *Edwards,* 107 S. Ct. 2573 (1987).
18. *Torcaso* v. *Watkins,* 367 U.S. 488 (1961).

Had I anticipated how the term *Secular Humanism* would be used, I would have kept my mouth shut and certainly would not have urged this argument or included it in my brief. I am sure that Justice Black, author of the Court's monumental opinion in the *McCollum* case (which barred religious instruction in public schools) would never have sanctioned such use.

For a quarter of a century "Secular Humanism" and Footnote 11 lay dormant. Then, they were suddenly rediscovered by Utah's Senator Orrin G. Hatch, and this is what happened.

In 1984 Congress adopted the Education for Economic Security Act for the purpose of bringing up to date the Higher Education Act of 1963 and the Elementary and Secondary Act of 1965. One provision of the new statute read: "Grants under the subchapter ["Magnet School Assistance"] may not be used for consultants, for transportation, or for any activity which does not augment academic improvement." With no public notice, Senator Hatch, chairman of the Senate's Committee on Education, tacked on to this proposed exclusionary subsection the words "or for any course of instruction the substance of which is secular humanism."[19] The subsection thus read:

> Grants under this subsection may not be used for consultants, for transportation, or for any activity which does not augment academic improvement or for any course of instruction the substance of which is secular humanism.[20]

At the time, however, a definition for *Secular Humanism* was difficult to find. In an interview reported in the February 22, 1985, issue of the *New York Times,* Senator Daniel Moynihan of New York said: "I have no idea what secular humanism is. No one knows. . . . I thought it was the price I had to pay to get

19. We should note that, unlike usage in the *Torcaso* v. *Watkins* footnotes, the words *secular humanism* are not capitalized here. Presumably, this was so because the words *consultants* and *transportation* also were not capitalized. This is quite logical, since if the term were capitalized as in the *Torcaso* footnote, the amendment would be unneccessary; *McCollum* v. *Board of Education* would forbid its devotional teaching in the public schools.

20. Since the Hatch amendment, the initial letters are sometimes capitalized and sometimes they are not.

desegregation money." Earlier, in the January 10, 1985, issue of the *Washington Post,* a press spokesman for Senator Hatch said that "secular humanism"

> is almost a term of art. You get into value education and a bunch of touchy-feely stuff that came out in the 70's. Conservatives object because these things may get in the way of a Christian education. . . . That's a long way of saying there is no quick definition of it.

Senator Hatch and his staff couldn't decide what a course using "secular humanism" might be; nor could his committee, nor could the Department of Justice attorney called in for assistance, so they decided to pass the ball to local school boards. "School boards," Senator Hatch's staff assistant explained,

> depend on sane, responsible people running them. There is no definition you can build into federal law that can keep crazy people from misinterpreting things. The absence of a working definition was a glitch. But with a little luck it won't be a serious glitch.

Accordingly, a resolution was adopted that read:

> A LEA [Local Education Agency] that receives [financial] assistance under this part may not use funds for any course of instruction the substance of which the LEA determines is secular humanism.

Unfortunately the glitch turned out to be more serious than Senator Hatch and his staff expected.

Unfortunate too, at least for nonfundamentalists, was the reality that the glitch would not go away. On the contrary, the publicity arising from newspaper accounts of the Hatch amendment resulted, on the one side, in a nationwide awakening among fundamentalists who suddenly realized that they had discovered a good thing and were not about to let it go; and, on the other side, it invoked the People for the American Way to call upon the Education Department to define what it meant by "secular humanism" in its regulation, and the American Jewish Congress to request that the department amend the regulation so as to make it clear that the act "does not authorize much less require public schools to urge religious values on their students."

Senator Hatch came to realize that the glitch had to be extinguished, preferably as publicly unnoticed as was its inception. Accordingly, a bill was introduced to amend the statute, deleting "or for courses of instruction the substance of which is secular humanism." The amended bill was passed in both Houses of Congress and approved by the president in November of 1985, a little more than a year after it was first enacted. *Sic transit* Hatch amendment.

Fundamentalists, however, could not be so easily disposed of. In one community a suit was brought by the mother of a public high school student in Washington state, seeking an injunction against inclusion in the English literature curriculum of Gordon Park's novel, *The Learning Tree*. The two sentences that the plaintiff and her daughter found to be offensive to their religious belief read:

> Newt found himself repeating after the bailiff,—"to tell the truth and nothing but the truth, so help me God." He asked strength of something, *be it God or whatever,* to carry him, his family or the rest of the colored people safely through the trouble he now imagined his testimony would bring. [Emphasis added.]

Mrs. Grove contended that requiring her daughter to read these two sentences violated the First Amendment's ban on laws respecting an establishment of religion. To support this claim she relied primarily on the *Torcaso* footnote. Use of the book, she said, had an effect of inhibiting her own religion, that of fundamentalist "Christianity," and at the same time of advancing "the religion of secular humanism."

The Federal Court of Appeals, however, ruled against her. "Secular humanism," the Court said, "*may be a religion,* but since the book was included in a review of English literature as a comment on American literature, its use does not constitute state establishment of religion or anti-religion."[21] Without stating any opinion, the Supreme Court rejected Mrs. Grove's appeal.[22]

Another case that is obviously an offspring of *Torcaso's* Footnote 11 (although that decision was not cited in the trial judge's opinion), is found in the case of *Mozert* v. *Hawkins County Public Schools*.[23] There, the plaintiffs, fundamentalist Christian school children and their parents, brought suit claiming that their religion required that the children not be exposed to the Holt, Reinhart and Winston reading book series in the county's public schools. They claimed that it was not one book but the entire sixth-grade series that contained material contradictory to their own religious beliefs. They believed that after reading the entire series a child might adopt the views of a feminist, a humanist, a pacifist, an anti-Christian, a vegetarian, or an advocate of a "one-world government," all of which would violate their religious beliefs and conscience.

In their suit the plaintiffs did not demand that these books be barred from sixth-grade use. Nor did they claim that the children had been denied the right, under Tennessee law, to opt out completely from the public school and avail themselves of a total curriculum in home schooling. They demanded only that the school authorities provide for these children an alternative reading series that did not contradict the plaintiffs' religious beliefs.

The plaintiffs based their suit upon the Free Exercise Clause of the First Amendment. The defendant school authorities, on the other hand, claimed that any attempts to provide acceptable textbooks for the plaintiffs would violate the First Amendment's Establishment Clause in that it would result in excessive state entanglement with religion.

The trial judge handed down what may be called a Solomonic decision. He denied the plaintiffs' demand for alternative in-school instruction based upon religiously acceptable books.

21. *Grove* v. *Mead School District*, 753 F. 2d 1528 (1985). [Emphasis added.]
22. *Grove* v. *Mead School District*, 106 S. Ct. 85 (1985).
23. *Mozert* v. *Hawkins County Public Schools*, 765 F. 2d 2975 (1985).

On the other hand, he held that the parents or their children could not be compelled to withdraw from the public school system to receive their education in private or non–state supported schools that provide instruction acceptable to fundamentalists. Instead, the judge ruled that during the reading instruction period the students would withdraw to a study hall or the library and would study acceptable literature with a parent later at home. From time to time the children's reading proficiency would be rated by the standardized achievement tests used by the state.

This opt-out plan, the judge ruled, would not contravene the Establishment Clause since there is neither state sponsorship nor active involvement of the state in religious activity. If deficiencies should develop the parents and school officials should confer to facilitate improvements. (Nothing is said in the opinion as to what would happen if the conference did not lead to a solution acceptable to both sides.)

The School Board, however, was not satisfied with this solution. On the same day that the decision was handed down, it filed a notice of appeal to the United States Court of Appeals. That court agreed with the board and unanimously reversed the District Court's decision. "If," one of the judges said, "the school district were required to accommodate exceptions and permit other students to opt-out of the reading program and other core courses with materials found objectionable, this would result in a public school system impossible to administer." In other words, if the courts were to eliminate everything that is objectionable to any sect or inconsistent with any of their doctrines, they would leave education in shreds. The plaintiffs sought to appeal to the Supreme Court but that Court refused to take their appeal.[24]

The *Mozert* case is far from unique. Similar cases are being brought before courts throughout the country, although mostly in the South. For example, the January 4, 1987, issue of the *Washington Post* magazine reported that in Panama City, Florida, the

24. 108 S. Ct. 1029 (1988).

public school authorities acceded to a parent's complaint that Susan Beth Pfeffer's book *About David*, relating the consequences of a sixteen-year-old high school student's shooting his adoptive parents and then himself, should no longer remain on the reading list. The plaintiff parent asserted that the subject of teen violence is best "handled prayerfully at home," with the use of a book that does not include a scene in which a grieving teenager questions the existence of God.

The consequences of accepting the "secular-humanism-is-a-religion" approach to the public school system are frightening. Thaddeus Stevens and Horace Mann, among others, had conceived of a free public school system in which children of all faiths—or no faiths—race, economic standing, and gender would be eligible to attend without preference or discrimination. Indeed, they deemed this variety of religions, races, economic standing, and gender to be of great value to all children if for no other reason than their inevitable mingling in adult life.

The Supreme Court's 1925 decision in the combined cases of *Pierce* v. *Society of Sisters* and *Pierce* v. *Hill Military Academy*[25] established the constitutional right of parents to send their children to nonpublic schools, with the result that a substantial percentage of Catholic (and to a lesser extent Protestant and Jewish) children left the public schools. The fear of racially integrated schools has caused and still causes many parents to exercise their privilege of removing their children from the public schools and sending them to private (religious and secular) schools that are practically free of blacks and Hispanic Americans who are very poor and cannot pay the tuition. Added to this are fundamentalists who may find all public school textbooks tainted with secular humanism and therefore offensive to their religious conscience. All of this, I suggest, can realistically result in the disintegration of public school education.

25. *Pierce* v. *Society of Sisters* and *Pierce* v. *Hill Military Academy,* 268 U.S. 510 (1925).

Sooner or later, the Supreme Court will have to meet the problems arising out of its *Torcaso* Footnote 11.

VI. "Cults" and "Cultism" under the Establishment Clause

For a decade or so a great fear of "cults" spread over the land, and while it has to some extent abated, its presence is still seen in the multimillion-dollar verdicts being handed down by juries in suits against these so-called cults. It has never been easy to define a cult. I have suggested that if it is something you like, it's a religion; if it is something you don't feel strongly about one way or another, it's a sect; but if it is something you fear and hate, it's a cult.

My concern with cults is in their relationship to the Establishment Clause as passed upon by the Supreme Court. For the purpose of this chapter, I will limit the discussion to a consideration of the 1982 Minnesota case of *Larson* v. *Valente*.[26] This dealt with what was, in the past decade, the most feared and hated of cults, that formed by Reverend Sun Myung Moon under the English title of Holy Spirit Association for the Unification of World Christianity, generally called the Unification Church, whose adherents were popularly called Moonies. Moon served a Federal penitentiary sentence for tax evasion in a situation that in instances too many to count is resolved in the Internal Revenue Office by payment of the due taxes together with an appropriate fine for late payment.

The *Larson* case involved a Minnesota statute that was enacted in 1978. Prior to that time, religious organizations were exempted from complying with a law requiring charitable organizations seeking contributions from the public to register and submit extensive annual reports to the State Department of Commerce. Among other things, the report had to state in detail

26. *Larson* v. *Valente*, 426 U.S. 228 (1982).

total receipts and income from all sources and the costs of management, fundraising, and public education.

The 1978 amendment established a "50 percent rule" in the exemption provision covering religious organizations. That is, only those religious organizations that received more than half of their total income from members or affiliated organizations were to be exempt. Further, a charitable organization was deemed ineligible to maintain its registration under the act if it expended for fundraising an "unreasonable amount," which was designated as 30 percent of its total income.

Shortly after the enactment of the 1978 law the Unification Church received notice from the department that it was required to register under that law. In return, members of the church and the church itself brought a suit challenging the constitutionality of the amendment. It was adopted, they asserted, as an assault upon the church (and similar cults) that, unlike established churches, in order to survive had to resort to contributions from nonmembers in excess of 50 percent.

The Supreme Court, upholding the lower court's decision, ruled in favor of the church. The 1978 amendment, it said, could not be justified under the Establishment Clause because it preferred some religions (those that were long-standing and thus able to maintain themselves without crossing the 50 percent line) over newly founded religions ("cults") such as that of the Unification Church, which could not survive without crossing that line. Moreover, the Court said, administration by the state of the 1978 amendment would result in impermissible entanglement of church and state. In sum, the state's action in this case could not be reconciled with the mandates of the Establishment Clause.

VII. Conclusion

One can understand Justice Rehnquist's unhappiness in *Wallace* v. *Jaffree* and that of the Reagan administration with the Court's interpretation and application of the Establishment Clause, particularly in the arena of education at the elementary and secondary school levels. The Court has rejected a great variety of efforts seeking to circumvent the *McCollum* decision barring religious instruction in the public schools, and the decisions in the *Engel* case and other cases banning prayer in those schools. Indeed, in later cases it extended the ban to encompass prayer not only during but also immediately before or after regular instruction takes place. Fundamentalist unhappiness with these decisions has manifested itself in a continuing outbreak of lawsuits and the establishment of unlicensed nonpublic schools, often utilizing nonlicensed teachers.

The situation is not substantially better in respect to governmental funding of nonpublic religious schools. The *Everson* decision allowed public financing of bus transportation to and from these schools, but the Court refused to extend this to encompass the funding of field trips during the school day to visit governmental, industrial, cultural, and scientific centers designed to enrich the secular studies of the students.[27] Similarly, the Court has refused to extend the *Board of Education* v. *Allen*[28] decision upholding use of public funds to finance the loan of secular textbooks for religious school use, to encompass the loan of other secular teaching materials and equipment such as projectors, record players, maps, and globes.[29]

Perhaps most encouraging to strict separationists are the Court's most recent cases. In the *Grand Rapids School District* case[30] it ruled violative of the Establishment Clause a public school district Shared Time and Community Education program that provided classes in schools that, but for the Shared Time programs, were used exclusively for religiously oriented (i.e., parochial) instruction. At the same time the Court, in *Aguilar* v. *Felton*,[31] invalidated as violative of the Establishment Clause a provision in the Federal Elementary and Secondary Act

27. *Wolman* v. *Walter,* 433 U.S. 229 (1977).
28. *Board of Education* v. *Allen,* 392 U.S. 236 (1968).
29. *Meek* v. *Pittenger,* 421 U.S. 349 (1975).
30. *Grand Rapids School District* v. *Ball,* 105 S. Ct. 3216 (1985).
31. *Aguilar* v. *Felton,* 105 S. Ct. 3332 (1985).

of 1965 that authorized use of Federal funds to pay the salaries of public school teachers engaged to provide remedial instruction in some secular subjects in parochial schools. Finally, as we have seen, in *Wallace* v. *Jaffree* the Court invalidated a statute requiring a moment of silent prayer in public schools before regular instruction begins.

Not that accommodation protagonists have been without victories. The Supreme Court, for example, has given publicly financed colleges and universities almost *carte blanche* in respect to religious instruction and prayer; it has refused to overrule the *Everson* bus transportation and the *Allen* textbook cases; and it has allowed income tax deductions for parochial school tuition payments, although not income tax credits.[32] All in all, however, one can well understand Justice Rehnquist's unhappiness with the Court's refusal to make the Establishment Clause almost a dead letter in American constitutional history. As of now, it can fairly be said that the Establishment Clause is alive and doing quite well. Whether this will continue to be the case with respect to a Court in which three members are Reagan's appointees, only time will tell.

If I may be allowed to make a hopeful prediction, I suggest that the Court will, in large measure, continue to rule unconstitutional what absolutists deem to be violative of the Establishment Clause. The basic relevant principles will survive; after all, this is what has happened until now in a Court in which all but two of the members were appointed by Republican presidents.

32. *Mueller* v. *Allen,* 463 U.S. 388 (1983).

Religion, Rights, and the Constitution

Max L. Stackhouse

We celebrated the bicentennial year of the Constitution for good reason. The television ad that speaks of the Constitution as "the single most important document in all our lives" may be an offense to any who take the Holy Scriptures seriously, yet it is a remarkable human achievement. Its authors offered solutions to four problems that have long vexed public affairs. The first is the problem of the one and the many. The states were reluctant to relinquish the degree of sovereignty that they held, yet the existing models for national unity had been the source of those ills that had caused many to come to this land. The development of a viable federal system allowed a new political vision of pluralism within unity.

The second problem is that of succession. For most of human history, succession was by dynastic connection, by palace intrigue, or by military might. Incompetence, insecurity, and injustice were the frequent results. The Constitution established a new system of governance in a republic with periodic change by episodic, direct, participatory democracy. Now, all over the world, any system that does not provide for regular, free, and open elections is viewed as backward and oppressive.

The third problem is distribution of authority. Every complex society has, and has to have, a variety of offices and functions to conduct public business. The most frequent way of ordering authority, in human history, has been vertical hierarchy. But such a structure invites both oppression from the top down and resentment from the bottom up. The people are roused to overthrow domination and a temporary passion of opposition becomes powerful. Such passion can destroy old elites, but can seldom construct a new order, without which populist solidarity degenerates into a chaos, which invites new tyranny (as the French Revolution was about to show again).

The authors of our Constitution distrusted hierarchy. They also feared the passions of majorities. They began the Constitution with "We the People" and they spoke of wanting "to form a more Perfect Union . . . ," but they immediately ordered that unity by breaking it up and giving it a structure in which those parts closest to the people were to be regulated by those protected from the changing whims of the people—especially the judiciary. They established a bicameral legislature and made it both distinct from and interlocked with the executive branch, all elected. No part of the whole could dominate other parts, *and* every surge of radical sentiment could find expression through elections, but still be constrained by counterbalancing order that tried to represent the perennial, the more constant, if not the eternal. Where mass movements have overthrown elites but have not established checks and balances of this kind, chaos or tyranny have quickly followed.

Fourth, they established a government of law and not of people. They wanted to reduce the arbitrary authority of leaders and the dependence of public life on the vagaries of personal character, breeding, or sentiment. They thought well-crafted institutions could reduce the effects of human evil and enhance the possibilities for human good.

I. The Public and the Private

For their contributions in these four ways, we can celebrate and honor the Constitution and its authors. But they did not solve all the problems. For instance, a perennial issue is the relationship of "public" to "private" matters. This problem is particularly dramatic in economic and family life. For most of human history, economic and political power was consolidated in the same set of hands, and those hands belonged to a specific family. The great revolutions were the displacements of an old dynasty by a new one. But at the time of our Revolution, Americans were clear that they did not want any royal family running polity or any government running the economy. They learned early what others have found out in more recent experiences of colonialism, fascism, and communism: When big bucks marry big guns, the little people pay for the wedding.

But that did not solve the problem for political and economic powers. They knew that governments print the money by which business buys, sells, and calculates; and producers generate the wealth by which governments fund all they do. They also knew that when economies fail, regimes fall, and when government collapses, economies fall apart. Yet, the logic of production and distribution of goods is not the same as the logic of the accumulation and exercise of power. Government makes a poor farmer and trader; business makes a poor magistrate and soldier. And family life suffers if it is based on considerations of either wealth or power.

In consequence, our forebears drew a rather sharp line between what is "public," by which they meant "governmental," and everything else, which they called "private." That distinction has produced the wealthiest society in human history. Indeed, it is the fruits of the economy which many identify with the American dream and with the American way of life. This has led to great ambiguity about the degree to which government should intervene in economic crises, as we have seen in the intense debates following "Black Tuesday" in 1929 and renewed again after "Black Monday."

Here we find the sharpest international criticism of what America stands for and the nucleus of our most intense internal debates. The division of public and private has allowed the development of economic institutions that seem to rival the government itself, but we blame government if the "private sector" fails.

We can perhaps see this most clearly in international affairs. We have two foreign policies, and we are unsure how they ought to be related. When we learned that a corporation had influenced the CIA to help overthrow a constitutionally elected democratic government in Chile some years ago, our sense of repugnance was wide and deep. Great damage was done. Democratic values appeared to be only masking economic interests. In a series of long public debates, it was agreed: the instruments of government should not be allowed to become instruments of corporate interest.

Still, the problem was not solved. More recently, we have witnessed the attempt by a member of government to establish foreign policy through a series of extragovernmental contacts, contracts, and corporations. The Irangate hearings have brought Americans to a second conclusion: public policy should not be made through private channels.

We know what we do not want; but we do not know what we want. We do not want the corporations running Washington and we do not want Washington running our business. Yet we also do not want an entirely unregulated economy, one in which corporate decisions and market forces determine the price of everything. And this way of stating things is structurally parallel to the issue of how much we want government to be related to a whole range of institutions that were not imagined by the authors of the Constitution. How much do we want government to regulate political parties, the interactions of social groups, and the operations of the universities, hospitals, and professions? All of these have grown up under the mantle of the "private" realm, all of them are indispensable to modern civilization, and none of them we want fully politicized or handed over to government bureaucracies.

Of special importance here is the family. It was, when the Constitution was being written, the central economic institution, the primary unit of production, distribution, and consumption, and the central social institution of daily life—as well as a divine institution established by God for the perpetuation of the human race, the formation of character, the expression of the affections, and the constraint of lust. The family continues to be a primary unit of consumption. But the corporation is the primary locus of production; the market is the primary center of distribution; and what is available for consumption is largely determined by forces outside the family. Nor is the family the only major social center for education, or medical care, or entertainment, or sexual behavior, as it once was. In many circles the sacredness of the family is seriously doubted. Quite often it is seen, on the analogy of a commercial contract, as a voluntary agreement between consenting adults, the terms of which are negotiable. And here we have the second great debate about the relationship of public and private in the contemporary world: defining the boundaries of privacy. There is insight in the current joke:

—"What do you think about the right to privacy?"
—"None of your damn business."

We can see something of the more serious problem in the debates over Robert Bork's nomination to the Supreme Court. Let us not claim that the days of heresy trials are over. These debates represent precisely the modern attempt to establish an orthodoxy, and therefore inevitably also a heresy, about the hermeneutical principles that are to guide our understandings of our Constitution regarding what is private and what is public.

In part this was simply a power struggle between liberals and conservatives, but it was more than that. It was a debate about how to interpret national sin and salvation. The chief difference between liberals and conservatives today has to do with their opposite assessments of the relationship of government to economic life and to family life—or, to put it more bluntly, of the relationship of power to money and sex. Liberals want more control over business and more freedom for sex; conservatives want more protection for "the family" and more freedom to make money. They draw the line of separation between public and private in different places for they see the threats of sin and the promises of salvation in different places.

Bork, as a scholar, has been a vocal critic of the modes of argument used by the Supreme Court to draw this line in a liberal direction in the last thirty years. As a judge, he actually drew the line in a way quite similar to the Court, but on other grounds. As a candidate for the Supreme Court, he became the symbol of a conservative, antiliberal perspective—especially to those who remember that kind of conservatism which made money at the expense of minorities and lynched blacks who were thought to threaten the white family. The general public, not much caring about how arguments are made, but very concerned with how they come out and basically pleased with key decisions made by the Supreme Court in the last thirty years, were persuaded that Bork was a threat to the liberal way of drawing that line. Ironically, the candidate who eventually was confirmed as justice, Judge Kennedy, appeared likely to make more conservative judgments on particular cases, but was not opposed so vigorously by the liberals because he did not challenge the prevailing hermeneutical principles. Journalistically speaking, the liberals won; in a broader historical perspective, the battle is quite undecided, for the hermeneutic by which we draw these lines remains confused and neither side deserves unambiguous regard. That is why, I suspect, nominations to the Supreme Court in the foreseeable future will be more "ideologically" interrogated than in the past.

II. Of First Principles

We honor the Constitution and the Bill of Rights for what they have provided—the creative reconstruction of common institutional arrangements, which allow us to debate the best distinctions between public and private. But in the final analysis, it is not the mechanics we most admire. What we most honor is the "metaphysical-moral vision" behind the Constitution. The Constitution was possible not only because it arranged an ingenious system, but because it embodied a "spirit." It gave institutional form to the first principles of social ethics to which Americans have appealed when they struggled to overcome the tyranny of colonialism in the eighteenth century, of slavery in the nineteenth, and of totalitarianism in the twentieth. If we can identify these first principles, we will begin to point to the marks of the spirit we seek, and to clarify the hermeneutic we need in law, politics, and life.

To be sure, the Constitution does not speak overtly of spiritual and ethical matters, and we cannot require confessional conformity with regard to these matters of all citizens or all public servants; but without them the Constitution would not have been written, and without grasping them, we cannot interpret what the Constitution meant or keep alive what it means. In the Bork hearings, we had a public debate about what the "spirit" of the Constitution is, about whether it can be grasped by statements of first principles so that they can become articulate in the governance of the common life, and whether "original intent," in the model of contract theory, is an adequate way of grasping what is at stake.

Here, I believe, we come to the deeper and unresolved issue that stands behind the hearings. Bork did not help us clarify what the first principles might be. He lost because he could not convince the committee or the public that he knew, for all his scholarship, what the foundations were for public interventions in areas of "private" economic life where civil rights were at stake, or for the restraint of intervention in arenas of sexual privacy that have in the past been under "public" scrutiny.

However, this is not a particularly admirable victory for liberals. Bork's opponents had only one alternative to his contractual version of "original intent." They appealed to "the spirit of the times," the point on which Judge Kennedy and Senator Kennedy basically agreed. But since Hegel, philosophically, and both Stalin and Hitler, politically, all appeals to the Zeitgeist are properly suspect. They might have appealed to the U.N. Declaration on Human Rights, for example, but they preferred the anomic sense of historicity. Their victory provided little sense of how an archaic document might be seriously read and interpreted when we are faced with new issues. In brief, the liberals showed no better hermeneutic than the conservatives.

Neither side seemed to realize that the basic issues of the Constitution are a mixture of religious, moral, and metaphysical presuppositions that, in combination, illumine the most reliable bases of public polity and policy. We may call that combination "public theology." What it points to is ignored (or held suspect) by the most influential theorists and by the most active groups of our day. Indeed, one crisis of America today is this: if we did not have the Constitution, we would not be able to write one because the most vigorous intellectual and sociopolitical forces today press in directions opposed to precisely those presuppositions that made the Constitution possible. They have, in many ways, been deconstructed.

I am not, of course, arguing that those who wrote the Constitution were consciously thinking of theology in the way it might be taught in a seminary or a Bible study group. I am suggesting that key presuppositions about God, the world, and the basic character of "covenant" (but neither *la contrat social* nor the Zeitgeist) provided the background beliefs of those who drafted the Constitution; that they had been vigorously debated for several centuries so that they had become "second nature"; and that they were shared by the people in the colonies enough that they would agree to accept what they rendered as true, just, and practicable.

III. What Frames the Constitution?

We can identify the presuppositions informing the Constitution, I think, by citing two sentences that are outside it but that historically and intellectually frame it. One sentence comes from the beginning of the Declaration of Independence: "We hold these truths to be self-evident; that all men are created equal; that they are endowed by their creator with certain unalienable rights; that among these are life, liberty, and the pursuit of happiness."

The second sentence is from the First Amendment to the Constitution. It reads: "Congress shall make no law respecting an establishment of religion, or prohibiting the free exercise thereof; or abridging the freedom of speech, or of the press; or the right of the people peaceably to assemble, and to petition the government for a redress of grievances." Here too we have the fruit of a public theological conviction—spelled out in its structural implications.

These are rather remarkable sentences. Their authors evidently knew that the construction of something enduring requires reliable acquaintance with metaphysical-moral foundations. The authors of the Constitution thought that the formation of the polity of a civilization depended on getting such things right and then building a workable, dynamic system to make such things possible in the common life.

It is quite possible that without the metaphysical-moral principles of the first, and the structural-organizational principles of the second, the Constitution would long since have passed away—as have efforts to develop constitutions in innumerable countries around the world where thinking of matters in this way is rejected.

More profoundly, if something like these principles are not valid, and hence deserve to be forgotten, then the reason for honoring the Constitution becomes moot, and the idea of constitutionalism as governance by laws rather than by arbitrary will and power proves to be a false one. We should then throw our energies into the naked struggle for power, for then everything private is politicized and politics becomes fateful for every private possibility. The strong, the rich, the unscrupulous will win, and nothing could or should constrain them.

If that is the way things really are, the quest for a reliable hermeneutic—in politics, in jurisprudence, in theology—is at best a ploy to mask private interests.

These two sentences, however, point theologically, jurisprudentially, and politically to matters that transcend interests;

and they are the clue to a viable hermeneutic. That is frightening to many, because it smacks of some kind of knowledge of "absolutes" and "universals." And today, although the existence of universals and absolutes is not denied, the human capacity to know anything about them is—universally and absolutely.

But note how universal and absolute this first sentence is: all are created equal; all are endowed by their creator with certain rights; these rights are unalienable; and these matters are self-evident. This set of truth-claims about the foundations of justice is a very high order. It is not religious in the sense of "We keep the Sabbath," or "I know that my Redeemer lives, for He lives within my heart"; these are theological claims about the metaphysical-moral foundations of the public world.

Of course, on the surface, it does not seem that all these things are all that universal or self-evident. They have not been acknowledged by everyone, everywhere; and large numbers of people, regimes, and traditions deny them regularly. These principles are only self-evident when things are seen from a particular angle—namely, the angle of God. And that is the point. It is a theological point of reference. It is not theological in an exclusive or privileged way. But it is a claim in that there is a proper angle by which to see the world if one is going to talk about the grounds upon which any enduring public polity has to be based and the hermeneutics of human governance is to be determined. It is the claim that there is a point of view, a transcendent one, not one required of all but one available to all, from which the most important guidelines for living in communities become self-evident. Any who look at matters from that point of view can begin to grasp the spirit and identify the first principles on which the common life can be based. Perhaps others, from other points of view, can see the self-evident moral principles this point entails also, but any who cannot see such self-evident principles are mistakenly looking at the world from a wrong angle.

Such claims are very strange to many. To some, it is not theology at all, for it says nothing about redemption or revelation. But it is theology; it is simply a public rather than a confessional theology. That is, it is that dimension of theology which is able to give public warrant for its positions and is able to give ethical foundations to the common life. For others, such claims are too strong: they seem so olympian, so presumptuous. But that may be deceptive. It may well be that this is a most humble position, precisely because it puts human interests and ideologies, human law and will, under a larger vision than humans themselves could construct.

IV. All Under God

Perhaps we can see this if we try to unpack some of the strands woven into this very thick public theological statement. Five points are most notable.

First, the Declaration refers to "all men." Some authors may have intended this in the generic sense; but it is doubtful. Those who signed the Declaration were surely thinking of propertied, white males. Certainly other laws that they penned excluded women, slaves, and those who were without property from the rights about which they wrote so beautifully.

Yet, it could be that the principles they discerned were more valid than their own understandings of them. It may well have been like much in both theology and jurisprudence—we only get glimpses of truth and we only walk on the boundaries of justice. But sometimes, in these glimmers and pilgrimages, we get clear enough and close enough to see that something really important is out there, even if we cannot possess it fully. Often we can only point to it with ambiguous language. In such moments, what we almost grasp is in principle more important than what we think we grasp and how we tell others about it. And that is what, I think, happened at this moment.

Certainly the greatest moral victories of this nation were to come in the next two centuries. The spirit of that basic principle became more and more incarnate when, bit by bit, the "all" began to triumph over the "men," when greater access to the same rights as held by propertied white males were extended in principle to nonpropertied men (in the Jackson era), to nonwhite people (in the Lincoln era), and to women (in the Roosevelt era).

In most areas of life, this story is still unfinished. It does not deny the reality of differences between people—in size, energy, intelligence, talent, strength, national origin, sex, age, race, susceptibility to diseases, and so forth. But all such differences are secondary from one perspective. When viewed from the standpoint of the Creator, we can catch a glimpse of the universal truth: All are equal. Nor is it only a "spiritual" equity; it is an equality that is to become socially incarnate in constitutional order: God wants equality of legal status for all. Whatever limits or prevents that can be altered.

Closely related is a second point: "All" does not refer to citizens in a nation-state only. It is more universal than that. The United States of America was not yet formed as a nation-state when the Declaration's authors wrote this sentence. They were not writing about those who were subjects of the government, and certainly not about subjects of the British crown. They were speaking, in the language of their day, of those matters that for centuries had been spoken of theologically: All people are under God, created by God, children of God, made in God's image. Human dignity is conferred by God—it is not established by governments, nor by agreements among the people, nor by the "spirit of the times." Were this the case, governments could repeal rights as easily as grant them, people could redraft their contracts ignoring such rights, or swallow them into new spirits of new times as the Zeitgeist changed.

The implications of this "All" are rather vast. On the basis of this "All" Americans fought and died in the twentieth century against tyrannies right and left. On the basis of this "All" we presume to try to defend movements and leaders and struggles that will enhance human rights in Central America, in South Africa, in the Mid-East, and in Asia. We may debate whom it is that we think most likely to aid, or threaten, the rights of all, but we have a common standard by which to assess the merits of our arguments. On the basis of this "All" we properly heed criticism of our own policies and behaviors at home and abroad.

103

This is the "All" that engendered the United Nations Declaration on Human Rights after a twentieth-century barbarism denied that all were equally under God and claimed that "natural" differences were more important.

The Declaration was very clear about this: "To secure these rights, governments are instituted. . . ." Governments and constitutions do not make human rights; they are instruments that can be changed or altered, accordingly as they are obedient to the rights of all humans. And that implies that any particular government is subject to standards that transcend any nation and every particular context, any people and every particular human quality. In other words, the foundations of the Constitution are internationalist in a way that the Constitution itself cannot be. Nation is thus always morally subject to humanity. Civil rights are always to be evaluated by human rights.

V. Universal Rights

The third point answers the question, what are these rights? "Life, liberty, and the pursuit of happiness," the Declaration says. Fascinating! In this phrase we can find a condensed version of the history of Western political theory. Aristotle had spoken for the classical tradition when he argued that the "natural end" of life is happiness. It is the duty of leaders, he said, to form virtue in the citizenry, which would bring all to the natural end of happiness. Theorists ever since have debated the nature of happiness—with no small amount of argument about its relationship to "pleasure," and the capacity of any political system to induce or regulate virtue or to guarantee happiness or the increase of pleasure over pain.

Modern thought rejected that classical tradition and turned to the view that the common life had to be based on "natural rights." Notice the shift—from natural ends to natural rights, both to be distinguished from natural laws as the scientists of the day talked about them. John Locke, whose thought was very influential among the authors of the Constitution, typified this view. He had argued that there were three basic natural rights: life, liberty, and property.

The authors of the Constitution modified both traditions. They did not think that the first principles to guide life could be found by turning to natural ends or to natural rights alone. They were too much influenced by biblical traditions to take these without modification. Human moral nature was fallen. The biophysical universe, creation, might be called "natural"; but the foundational principles to guide life were God-given. They were part of God's covenant with humanity, and they included the gift of life and the right not to be under oppression and exploitation. But they also included another arena. What might that be if it is not happiness by state-guided virtue, or pleasure, or property?

An alternative understanding of happiness, which even our Deist forebears inherited from the biblical tradition, was the notion of the kinds of "happiness" or "blessing" that derive from meditation on God's law. The joy brought by this could in no way be guaranteed or engineered by any state. Nor could it be attained by the pursuit of pleasure. This was gained only by those who sought a new disciplined life on higher grounds. It was on this basis that the American, semi-secularized products of Jewish and Christian traditions modified the philosophical traditions that were so intellectually powerful. They added "the pursuit of happiness" to "life" and "liberty." To be sure, "property" is linked to "life" and "liberty" in the Fifth Amendment, but it appears there in the context of limitations on punishments in criminal procedure and on what may be taken from private hands for public use without just compensation. The main point is that at the decisive level of basic background beliefs, which were only vaguely in the forefront of conscious intent, life and liberty are combined neither with property nor with happiness nor with pleasure, but with the right to pursue blessedness. Thus it simultaneously limits absolutist claims to private property, to private pursuits of pleasure, and to the public attempt to guarantee happiness by engineering virtue. It is not another way of saying we have life or freedom as a right; it is a way of safeguarding a higher quest for a higher justice, transcending every government and, indeed, every pleasure and human virtue. That is, indeed, why we have life and liberty.

If we miss this point in noting these transformations of great secular political traditions of the West, we fail to see a very important point: life, freedom, and even the pursuit of happiness do not, perhaps cannot, stand on their own. They rest on a metaphysical-moral reality that stands on a foundation beyond the ordinary experience of life. That is why these rights are unalienable.

The human rights all people have, and the moral order on which they rest, are true and just in a way that experience seldom is. In fact, the issuing of the Declaration and the writing of the Constitution were done precisely because the Americans were not experiencing what they knew to be true and just. This is a rather amazing insight to a generation that believes that if something is not experience-based, it must be fantasy or imagination or false abstraction, one that thinks a trump consists of "In my experience. . . ."

But perhaps we should repair to ideas held by other generations—including the one that wrote the Constitution. People and institutions do not experience first principles all the time. Much of our experience of rights is in the breach of them; much of the moral order on which we rely is known only in a broken, fragmented, and fallen way. But the experience of untruth or injustice does not refute the validity of first principles; it makes them all the more necessary. Nor does the absence of a system to protect these principles mean that one may not be imagined. Indeed, we do not change the basic principles of truth and justice when they go against experience; nor do we void institutional life when it fails to protect these principles. Instead we rearticulate the principles as best we can and reconstruct the system of courts and constitutions and procedures to remedy experience so that it may be more true and just. And we seek the kind of people to work in these institutions who grasp these principles above all other things, and who can help form systems to make these principles come to experienced actuality.

These points all entail the view that humanity lives under

a basic moral design, if seldom according to it. To say that this design is given by God is to say that we did not invent it, and that there are limitations as to how humans ought to modify it, even if we develop the technical capacity and social will to do so. It also means that in the final analysis the precise character of this order is veiled in mystery. We humans may never know it very perfectly, and thus must be quite cautious in trying to specify all details of it prematurely.

These points also entail the belief that we can glimpse the contours of this reality well enough to catch something of its spirit, and we can know enough about the first principles to tell the difference between decent and indecent arguments with regard to it. Therefore, we have a basis by which we can construct open systems, a basis on which to deconstruct constricted systems, a basis on which to engage in the formation of reasonable systems, a basis for the reformation of irrational systems, and a basis on which to apply the more universalistic discernments of the past to the particular confusions of the present. In other words, we can draft Constitutions on this basis, and we can modulate laws when they are in discord with what we can know.

In brief, if this is true, we have the possibility of developing a hermeneutic for the common life. A public theology is key to it.

VI. Institutional Limits

But thus far, we have only dealt with the first set of issues that, I believe, frame our Constitution. Let me turn now to that second sentence, which also frames that which we celebrate: the First Amendment to the Constitution.

"Congress shall make no law respecting an establishment of religion, or prohibiting the free exercise thereof; or abridging the freedom of speech, or of the press; or the right of the people peaceably to assemble, and to petition the government for a redress of grievances."

Note the difference of level between what is in this sentence and what was in the previous one. There we saw the inevitable influence of theology on political life. Here we see a rather rigid institutional separation of church and state. This difference in level is important. Indeed, it is quite likely that the positive relationship between religion and politics at one level makes a negative relation possible—and necessary—at the other level. And it works the other way around: the negative organizational limits allow positive moral relationship.

The core reason for such distinctions is that, in the final analysis, humans are not saved by politics. Politics is a necessary human activity; public service is a high calling; governance may well be a gift and demand of God, and the pious of all religions may well be called to pray with thanksgiving for the relatively just, relatively peaceful, and relatively orderly governments possible in human history. But the state cannot save us. It can preserve us from some kinds of chaos, invasion, and crime; but it cannot ultimately guide our destiny or tell us what is worth living for or dying for. That requires modes of thought, discourse, and relationship that cannot be engendered or controlled politically.

When lawyers and legislators think of the First Amendment, they often divide the religious part from the other parts. Freedom of speech and of the press, and the rights to assemble and petition the government are dealt with separately from the two religious clauses—one preventing establishment and one permitting free exercise—as if the sentence were a string of beads, each one precious but quite unconnected from the next one. But historically, sociologically, politically, and theologically such a view simply does not work. Who was it, historically, who had fought for the right of free speech? What social organizations had fought for the right of access to the press, and the freedom to print and distribute their views? Who felt compelled to assemble peaceably? Who had been denied that right, and had challenged the authority of government over the issue? Who had been petitioning government because of grievances and been persecuted for doing that? The answer is clear: religious organizations—not all of them, of course, but specifically those churches that fought for disestablishment of religion as a basic implication of their belief in the absolute freedom of the church to form a disciplined order and seek God's blessing independent from government control.

We should remember that the Constitution refers to only a few organized groups besides the government itself—foreign nations, the states, and Indian tribes. No reference is made to political parties, universities, newspapers, or publishing houses. Nor are there any references to corporations or families. All these things could be politically, governmentally, managed. The remarkable first sentence in the Bill of Rights offers the only institutional safeguard for the social pluralism that the whole Constitution presupposes. This provision alone gives explicit recognition to the right of nonofficial groups to organize, to speak, to assemble, to distribute their views, to pursue their deepest interests, and to influence the public. And it is the church that provided the institutional rock on which all other "Non-Governmental Organizations" (NGO), as the UN now calls them, are grounded. To be sure, the authors thought that there might well be state-controlled religion in the states of the union, and it was not until the 1830s that their vision of pluralism at the federal level was applied to the states; but the principle was here established.

VII. Institutional Rights

The distinctive organizational feature of pluralistic, constitutional democracy, as compared with tribal, feudal, monarchical, or totalitarian societies, is the open possibility for what specialists call "intermediary organizations," "voluntary associations," "mediating institutions," or "mezostructures." Every state recognizes, in some way, the existence of individuals; most speak explicitly of individual freedoms. But here we have something more. Individual freedom is a wonderful thing in many regards; but individuals can be ignored or marginalized one by one where these organized groups are not present. No one can ultimately control what is truly individual anyway, except by killing or imprisoning people (although torture is the supreme effort in this direction). It is no small thing to recognize individual freedom of expression and conscience; but in one sense, these cannot be forbidden or controlled anyway. In the privacy of a jail cell, even the torture victim can say "to hell with you" about the torturer. In consequence, totalitarian regimes often acknowledge the freedom to hold all sorts of beliefs—religious, ethical, political, or whatever—so long as they remain fully private.

What is remarkable about the First Amendment is that it recognizes that individuals may work in concert, in public, in assembly, in attempts to persuade others by speech and publication and petition of their claims about truth and justice. Organizations protect individuals from collective tyranny and from private isolation where conscience makes no difference. They combine individual resources so that truth can be sought, justice discussed, voluntary cooperation established, and actions taken on the behalf of persons. Thereby real freedom can be claimed. Such groups also help individuals to order their lives in communities of shared conviction and mutual support, without coercion, so that individuality does not become pathological.

Religion is not, after all, only beliefs and practices held by individuals; nor is it only theology and truth-claims. It is also, if it endures beyond a fleeting ecstatic moment, an ordering of community. And politics is not only about constitutional divisions of labor and principles of procedure, it is about power— the power to coerce, to control, to command, to tax, to regulate (as much of the Constitution discusses—to the boredom of every high school student who has to study it). Both cases entail an incarnate polity, an embodied institution.

In this context, the importance of the "separation" of church and state organizationally is very difficult to overestimate. It is the foundation of the separation of state and academia, of state and press, of state and profession, of state and union, and, in distinct and disputed ways, of state and corporation and of state and family. All of these are simultaneously public and private, even if they are not government and not individual. And here too we find several implications that are indispensable for a viable complex society.

First, this amendment to the Constitution acknowledges the existence of an arena of discourse, activity, commitment, and organization for the ordering of life over which the state has no authority. It is a remarkable thing in human history when the authority governing coercive power limits itself. It forces us to imagine what must have prompted, and legitimated, such an action. However much government may become involved in regulating various aspects of economic, technological, medical, cultural, educational, and even sexual behaviors in society, religion is an arena that, when it is doing its own thing, is off limits. This is not only an affirmation of the freedom of individual belief or practice, nor only an acknowledgment that the state is noncompetent when it comes to theology, it is the recognition of a sacred domain that no secular authority can fully control. Practically, this means that at least one association may be brought into being in society that has a sovereignty beyond the control of government.

Second, this amendment means a certain pluralism is inevitable in society. If no religion is established, and since everyone has always known that where one is not established several will develop since there is always more than one understanding of even a single religion, no monolithic structure is possible. Religion, in other words, cannot become a matter of state. This provision for the freedom of religion, implying the separation of church and state, has made the pluralistic society free also for the synagogue, the mosque, the temple, and, indeed, the cell, the caucus, and the party. And if any of them want to be effective and influential in the long run, they will have to work at the other level—that is, they will have to develop a public theology that is persuasive, universal, inclusive, and accessible to all, or it will not, and should not be, heeded in public discourse.

The religious accumulation of influence by the use of public power is restricted, just as is the use of coercion in the formation of religious community, for authority in the religious sense and legitimacy in the political-legal sense are divided at the level where violence or the threat of it might be employed. At this level, sin and crime are also distinct; the state may ignore what organized religion encourages and organized religion may deem sinful what the state allows. The privileges and duties of citizenship and those of religious membership are to be disengaged. Of course, they may overlap, and they do so frequently; but one may not serve as the mark of the other, and excommunication in one does not imply excommunication in the other.

Thus we must understand society as an association of associations (at least two of them, but that also functionally implies others such as family, sanctified by the church, or hospital, school, or workers' movement founded by it) wherein all forms of power—force, influence, legitimacy, and authority—can never be officially consolidated into one set of hands. The destiny of one is not inevitably tied to the destiny of the other. A regime may falter or fail, as they often do, but organized religion does not thereby cease to be. A church, denomination, sect, or cult may rise or die, become fanatical or vacuous, as sometimes happens (right in front of our eyes on TV), but that is not a crisis of state. No regime exists without the influence of religion on its political theory; but civilizations that identify religious and political institutions and make them a part of the same organized system make for bad politics—and bad theology.

Finally, the fact that religious institutions and all NGOs operate without state support or state control means that they have to live by the power of persuasion. People have to be convinced that what these groups are about is valid and valuable, or they will not follow what they teach, go to their meetings, or contribute their resources. Of course, various religious advocates can exert all kinds of pressure on people—emotional thrills and spiritual terrors, threats of divine exclusion or promises of divine acceptance. But they have to convince people in their hearts and minds that what they are talking about is godly and reasonable, or all this religious stuff will be thought to be simply fantasy and craziness.

VIII. Some Implications

The implications for problems we now face begin to become clear. We have an area where the line between public and private is drawn, and drawn very clearly. That is the model by which these things have to be argued. If matters are not to be ordered by the state, they have to sustain their freedom by demonstrating that they obey a higher order. We face, however, a new context in which both wealth and sexuality are increasingly thought to be organizationally independent from any norms established by state or church, or indeed from structures of corporate or familial accountability. Contemporary liberals and conservatives want to claim a new absoluteness of liberty in one or the other of these areas beyond the reach of the state's justice or divine righteousness; and those contemporary liberals and conservatives who are most vigorous in their advocacy of these freedoms are the least interested in developing the public theological-hermeneutical principles by which we can sort out the implications of human rights and social order in these areas.

It is doubtful theologically that individual behavior regarding the disposition of wealth and sex reflects the same kind of sacred sovereignty that religion does—or, for that matter, that freedom of the press, of expression, and of assembly does. When property is held in trusteeship, by incorporated stewards of the common good of the commonwealth, it should be given wide latitude. And when sexuality takes place within the sacred confines of marriage, we want to keep cops away from the bedroom door. In other words, government must give these communities of discipline, responsibility, and accountability wide berths of freedom. But when the God-given rights to life, liberty, and the pursuit of happiness are threatened by arbitrary exercises of private freedom—destroying the environment or aborting babies, exploiting labor or communicating AIDS, for example—the matters may be public in the governmental sense. And the guidelines about precisely how to draw the boundary between public and private as such question arise is first and foremost a matter of public theology, and hence of social ethics, jurisprudence, and legislation. They require a hermeneutic of first principles by which we interpret both the Constitution and the sociopolitical contexts of our common life.

This puts an enormous burden on religious leadership, and at present it is not doing very well on such questions. It is little wonder that many people who are concerned about public life and public discourse pay little attention to what clergy and theologians talk about, except in anxiety lest they become influential. Nor is there much wonder that many see the issues simply as a power struggle. This also puts a burden on the citizenry. We have to discern which kinds of theological principles are genuinely public and how we want them to be applied in the perennial necessity of making an ancient document pertinent to contemporary life. In other words, citizens have to become skilled at hermeneutics and at the relationships of first principles to polity and policy.

It is questionable whether we have a Constitution that can endure if the people are not convicted about the validity of the principles on which it is based. And we cannot have that conviction unless we can see the validity of the theological foundations on which these principles rest. That, above all, is the most pressing question for us if we are to honor the bicentennial of this Constitution in a way that will extend its blessings into the next century.

The Influence of Religion in America— More, Less, or What?

Harvey Cox

Hardly any question has surfaced with such force and persistence in recent years in America as that of the proper relationship between religion and public life. There are, of course, discussions about the right balancing of the branches of government, about the power of the courts to construe the basic law; about the correct relationship of the states to the federal government; and many other issues. However, the vital debate on these questions is virtually drowned out, it seems, by the number and intensity of arguments about the appropriate role religion should play in the formation of public policy in America.

The underlying assumption of this chapter is that one reason the question of religion and politics has loomed so large in recent years is what appears to be a massive and unanticipated reentry of religious influence in the public domain. I hedge my thesis by saying "what appears to be" since there is an active discussion now going on about whether the influence of religion ever in fact declined, or whether it simply went relatively unnoticed (or unreported) for a number of years or decades and has now come in for more press and scholarly attention. Some claim

115

that religion has always been a significant force in American public life and that what has happened recently is merely the effort of religious institutions to reassert a more "normal" state of affairs in response to a series of laws and court decisions that these spokesmen claim have wrongly curtailed the place of religion in our common life.

I will not seek to resolve this dispute here, but will assume that all the theories are partially true. Surely religion has played a large role in American history, as any serious student of that history must notice. Also, there has been a certain resurgence in religious activity in the public realm in America—the rise of the Religious Right, the Roman Catholic Bishops' Pastorals, the Rainbow Coalition—but some of this activity has definitely come in response to what its advocates define as an attack on religion by the courts and other branches of government. In my view, therefore, religion has never been as absent from the public policy realm as many of its critics now argue and what we are seeing is, in part at least, a genuine resurgence.

Furthermore, we can understand this resurgence of religion in American society only as part of a worldwide phenomenon. It is not at all restricted to American life but is to be seen in its variegated forms on all of the continents of the globe. I also want to argue that it is a highly ambiguous phenomenon. It presents a mixed picture not only for those committed to democratic institutions, free inquiry, and freedom of expression but also for those committed to the health and vitality of religion itself. I am presenting therefore three major points about the current role of religion: 1) that it is a global phenomenon; 2) that it was largely unanticipated by observers and critics; and 3) that it is both good news and bad news. I further want to ask about each of these assertions a more fundamental question, namely, why? *Why* is it worldwide? *Why* was it unanticipated? and *Why* is it (or, *What* makes it) so ambiguous?

I. A Worldwide Phenomenon

If one were to fly around the globe today, it would be difficult to land anywhere where a reemergence of religion into public life and cultural creation has not taken place in recent years. Let us begin where it all began: in the Holy Land where the fond hopes of those who wanted to found a state that would encompass both Jews and Palestinians have seen their hopes shattered. The pioneer Zionists who came to Israel to forge a new experiment in humanistic socialism have also watched their dreams come to naught. Today a powerful tide of Jewish fundamentalism is rising in the state of Israel and is a power to be contended with by all political parties. Recently ten thousand Israelis gathered at the Wailing Wall to insist there be no theatrical performances in Israel on Friday nights. The Gush Enumin is a significant factor in Israeli daily life—and it is not the only superconservative religious stream flowing. Moving north a few miles to Beirut, the global traveler would have to view with dismay the shattered wreckage of a state whose brilliant promise as a multi-religious society also seems to have failed. Not only do Christians fight Muslims, but within each of these camps a bitter internecine warfare rages on. Just to the east in the heart of the Muslim world the struggle between Sunni and Shi'ite continues. Riots break out in Mecca at the site of the Holy Kabba, and pilgrims are shot or trampled to death. On the other hand, throughout the Muslim world there is a feeling of rebirth and reawakening after centuries of domination by infidel colonial powers. Some Muslims contend that despite their current internal difficulties, the religious future of the world belongs to those who follow the command of Allah.

India presents one of the most troubling commentaries on the global reemergence of religion. Just as the country was celebrating the fortieth anniversary of its independence in August 1987, its leaders had to concede that the reappearance of communal and religious strife is a cause for deep worry. Muslims have been challenged to exert more influence within India in part by the renewed separatist activity of Sikhs. This in turn has

117

called forth a new kind of Hindu nationalism with all the resultant confrontation and violence. Also, the Hindu community itself has experienced increased antipathy and outbreaks of blood-letting between and among the various castes. Indeed, Dr. Sudhir Kakar, a noted Indian psychiatrist and the author of several books about the Indian character, explains: "As always India is facing a set of contradictions." Speaking of the accusations of scandals that have rocked his country, Kakar says, "The idea that corruption might reach up to the prime minister really shakes the Hindu idea of polity, where the god or ruler is the embodiment of divine order and the fount of integrity." Describing the communal and religious violence, Kakar says, "This is the thing that troubles me most. What it spells is an inevitable increase in violence involving religious communities." He then makes an instructive comment: "Secularism was one of our pillars, but it is hollow now." In an age of resurgent religion, where the resurgence is being greeted so positively by so many, it is significant to find a thoughtful Indian hankering for the "good old days" of secularism.

India is not the only place where the resurgence of religion is viewed with alarm. In Northern Ireland, parts of Africa, and Sri Lanka, confrontations between classes, tribes, and language and ethnic groups often are exacerbated by a religious factor.

The face of resurgent religion, however, is not always so grim. Sometimes it is hopeful and positive. Recent commentators on the Soviet Union have mentioned the remarkable new interest in spirituality found among Soviet intellectuals, especially in Leningrad and Moscow. Recent works of Soviet poets, filmmakers, and novelists are replete with discussions of religious and theological themes. The most widely celebrated new Soviet movie, "Repentance," which won a special prize at Cannes, ends with a cryptic conversation between an old woman and the young heroine about where the road of life leads and what good it is if it doesn't lead to a church. Meanwhile the Soviet novelist, Chingiz Aitmatov, has written a widely discussed novel called *The Executioner's Block,* in which he creates a kind of modern Soviet Christ figure named Abdias Kalistratov, who seems to many critics to be modeled after Prince Myshkin of Dostoyevski's *The Idiot.*

Religion is hardly dead in the rest of the Soviet empire. In Poland the continuing vigor of the Catholic Church impresses every visitor. The Polish church has become the host and patron for a wide range of cultural activities—plays, music, and poetry reading—within a society where the Communist government has completely lost the people's confidence.

We could go on to mention other parts of the world, including Japan where a rebirth of both local and state Shinto has completely mystified those who believed Japan was becoming the most secular of all the modern urban industrial states. We could also mention China where apparently thirty-five years of isolation from the rest of the Christian world has not sapped the Chinese Christian church of its vitality. On the contrary, it has more than doubled, perhaps even quadrupled its size over these years, relying mainly on small congregations meeting in the homes of believers.

I rehearse all these familiar phenomena so that we do not discuss the resurgence of religion in America or its meaning as though it were some isolated movement. It is part and parcel of a much larger and more comprehensive picture, and this leads us to ask our questions about its meaning in a more inclusive way.

II. An Unanticipated Phenomenon

When I was writing *The Secular City,* which was published in 1965, there seemed to be a consensus among almost all scholars and sociologists of religion that the role of religion in the *public realm* was in eclipse and would continue to decline. The reigning developmental theory in that era had been sketched out by Walt Rostow in his *Stages of Economic Growth.*[1] Some theologians talked about a post-Christian era, others about the death of God.

1. Walt W. Rostow, *Stages of Economic Growth: A Non-Communist Manifesto* (New York: Cambridge Univ. Press, 1960).

The Italian sociologist, Sabino Acquaviva, wrote, "From the religious point of view, humanity has entered a long night that will become darker and darker with the passing of the generations, and of which no end can yet be seen."[2] Those analysts who foresaw some role for religion in the future insisted that at least it would have no role in the *public* domain, but would have to eek out its existence in family rituals, among occasional ethnic groups, and perhaps in the interior life of individuals. Dag Hammarskjöld, General Secretary of the UN, was taken to be a kind of prototypical modern religious man. He apparently had a rich, internal mystical life, and kept a diary about it, but never talked about it with his colleagues and never seemed to allow it to spill out into his public role. That diary, *Markings*, published posthumously, was the first indication even some of his close acquaintances had of Hammarskjöld's spirituality. Religion, it was argued, had not died: it had simply evolved into an entirely inner "secret discipline." *Public* religion was finished.

This widespread consensus about the decline of religious influence in the public sector has (as we have seen in our global survey) turned out to be considerably less than accurate. But why? I think the mistaken forecast was a symptom of the unidirectional and universal model of development that held sway twenty-five years ago. The various theories of economic development that informed so much social planning and political strategy in the 1950s and 1960s taken together can be seen as one of the last truly comprehensive theories of human life to have emerged before the brutal facts of life and poststructuralist criticism began to render all such theories suspect. There is something a little odd about this. In the 1960s many thought we were living in a time beyond the great theories of civilization. Spengler and Toynbee were dead. We were also told by Daniel Bell and others that it was a time "beyond ideology."

But were these obituaries premature? The fact is that the development theories themselves constituted a philosophy of

2. Sabino Acquaviva, *The Decline of the Sacred in Industrial Society*, translated by Patricia Lipscomb (New York: Harper & Row, 1978), p. 201.

civilization, and an implacably sweeping and universal one at that. All societies, *without exception,* they declared, would inevitably be drawn into the vortex of economic development by the power and attraction of the world market. Furthermore, the stages of economic growth were fixed and immutable. All the people of the earth were headed toward the final stage of this ladder even though they were at various rungs at the time. Today it is hard to find anyone who will defend this remarkably comprehensive and universal schema.

The development theories were also unidirectional. They saw time as the flight of an arrow and allowed no possibility for regression, collateral movement, or circling. In some ways the modern development theories represent a secularized version of the biblical and Western idea of a history that begins, gathers everything into its movement, and moves inexorably toward a previously determined climax. Obviously some of the instances of resurgent religion I have already noted give the lie to this unidirectional thinking. The global economic planners did not foresee the Ayatollah Khomeini. Many believed that one could not have a modern industrial-technological society and also keep to the old rituals. Yet today we see Shinto priests lighting the sacred fire in a new Toshiba factory. On the other side of the world we find zealous Shi'ite Muslims fully capable of utilizing the latest military hardware and software in their struggle against those they consider heretics in their own family of faith. Apparently technology and religion go together more easily than these predictions had assumed.

There is another reason, however, why the worldwide phenomenon of resurgent religion was so unanticipated. It is because "modernity" is itself a meaning and value system. It is, in one sense, a "religion." It has its own doctrines, some explicit and some implicit, of who I am, what the good is, what history is about, and what human destiny will be. There has been much discussion recently about the term *postmodern,* and much of it has been dismissive. How can any age be postmodern, it is asked, when "modern" simply refers to the age in which we now live, whenever that age begins or ends. There is something to

121

these criticisms. But I believe that the term *postmodern* has important symbolic significance. It suggests that the "modern age" is not the final vantage point from which all others can be viewed and judged. It is not the summit of human development from which we can survey previous way stations and temporary base camps. Modernity is nothing more and nothing less than one cluster of values and meanings among other such clusters. *Postmodern* is largely a formal term that carries no particular content (or carries such different contents in various contexts as to make it virtually unusable). Nevertheless, it is a helpful reminder that our modern age is only one among others, not the *summum beatum.*

The "modern age" (Neuzeit) always defined itself in some measure with reference to what it called "religion." As the German theologian, Trutz Rendtorff, has demonstrated in a recent article in the *Journal of Religion,* religion was the "other" over against which the modern age declared its own identity. Of course, not all "modern" thinkers agreed on religion. Most thought it would be superseded sooner or later. Others thought a struggle should be carried on against its hegemony. Still others thought it needed to be purged and renovated in light of the assumptions of something they called the "modern mind." Much of the agenda of modern theology was the reformulation of religious claims into the language and thought forms of modernity. It is wrong to say, as conservatives frequently do, that this was always a "collapse" before modernity. Modern Christian theologians, for example, saw themselves *using* the language of modernity to make the gospel better known in the modern world. Nonetheless, the reinterpretation of religion in the light of modernity provided the main task for nearly two centuries of modern Christian theology.

It is important to note that one of the assumptions of modernity that was widely accepted by religious scholars and theologians during the heyday of modern theology was the habit of speaking of "religion" in the singular. It was always "religion," not "religions." It is easy to see why this usage developed. The "modern then know" had included *all* religious traditions in a single phenomenon called "religion" with reference to which they defined their own project. So theologians began doing the same. The theological assumption was that by interpreting, defending, or grounding a *particular* religion—usually my own—I was doing a service for *all* religion. Notice that Friedrich Schleiermacher entitled his famous work *On Religion: Speeches to Its Enlightened Despisers.* Schleiermacher does not say that he intends to defend a certain type of pietistic European Protestant Christianity against the criticisms of its educated nay-sayers, but that is in fact what he did. He, like his generations of followers, had accepted the "singularization" of religion.

The operative assumption in most modern religious thought since Schleiermacher is that religion can, in fact, be spoken of in the singular: that it is a unitary fundamental human phenomenon of which there are—of course—historical variants. Religion is "a deep structure of which the 'various religions'" of the world are local idioms. This assumption about the singularity of religion is one of the most pervasive in all of modern Christian theology. It undergirds, for example, most of the "farm development" theories. But it is also one of the most misleading assumptions. It has led to a subtle, if unintended, form of Christian imperialism. It has prevented Christian theologians from giving sufficient attention to the genuine pluralism and the autonomy and individuality of the various faith traditions of the world. Just as a "stages" theory of economic development proved invalid in many parts of the world, a stages theory of development may eventually prove to be equally provincial.

In any case, the "religion" of modernity, the value and meaning system that grew out of the Enlightenment and the capitalist organization of society and spread around the world, is now in decline. It is in decline for a wide range of reasons, including the economic and political senility of some of its major bearers—reasons too complex and numerous to enter into here. Consequently, one can accurately report that the surrogate faith-system that modernity created commands less and less credence in much of the world today. Some of its major tenets—

the supremacy of rationality, the role of the individual, the importance of the nation-state, the promise of science—now find themselves relentlessly questioned and sometimes discarded. Instead of the death of God, what we witness is the rebirth of the gods. What advertised itself as a universal and unidirectional system is breaking apart—and the responses to its demise are universal and unidirectional. If this description seems to suggest that we are entering a dangerous period of world anarchy and lack of cohesion, that may well be the case. But such fears cannot put the Humpty Dumpty of global modernity back on the wall. What we have is a worldwide resurgence of religious activity of a wide variety, united only by a common opposition to "the modern world" in one of its many different expressions.

III. The Resurgence of Religion Is Ambiguous

Are we witnessing a true resurgence of religion or merely noticing a subterranean stream that has resurfaced? However we answer that question, the fact is that, whatever it is, it is both good news and bad news. No one can survey the endless car bombing in the once proud "secular city" of Beruit, or the communal mayhem of India, or the increasing clout of Israeli fundamentalists, without longing, as does Dr. Sudhir Kakar, for a little good old-fashioned secularization.

Yet there is another, and better, side, as we have seen. One sign of this is the almost miraculous transformation of the Roman Catholic Church in Latin America. Not too many years ago that church was firmly allied to the feudal elites and aristocratic land owners of a desperately poor and often benighted continent where illiteracy, poverty, and hunger reigned. In the last twenty years large segments of that church's leadership— including hundreds of bishops, thousands of priests and sisters, and most of the theologians—have moved dramatically toward the support of the poor and the marginalized as the right social location for the Christian church on their continent. One could argue that the transformation of the Catholic Church in Latin America is at least in part attributable to the global upsurge of religion and to the renewal in the Catholic church itself which came to particularly dramatic expression at the Second Vatican Council. It is also true that the movement from the periphery into the arena of history being made by the marginalized peoples of the world has also caused this change within the Catholic Church. Gustavo Gutiérrez, one of the principal founders of the theology of liberation, says such a movement could have occurred only where the people were both very oppressed and very Christian. In any case, the "conversion" of the Catholic Church in Latin America is not something that has been done to or for the people, but is something they have done themselves. The title of a recent book by Leonardo Boff says it well. In an obvious allusion to the Gospel of John's statement about the Word becoming flesh, the book is called *E a Igaja se fez Povo* ("And the Church Became People"). I also count the increasing interest in religion in Communist countries as a positive sign, perhaps betokening the widespread inability or unwillingness of the people of those countries to continue to affirm that particular variant of the Enlightenment faith, the religion of modernity that Soviet-style Marxism eventually became.

In the U.S. the ambiguity of the return of religion reaches its culmination. This is the case in part because the religious traditions of this nation are so various and so vigorous. Consequently I want to mention a couple of positive outcomes of the growing influence of religion on the public realm and then mention a couple of more negative possibilities.

First, the joining of the debate about such issues as nuclear weapons and the purpose of our economy—as this was so effectively done by the Roman Catholic bishops of North America in their recent encyclicals—helped enlist larger numbers of people in a necessary public debate over key public questions. The Catholic bishops did everyone a favor by reminding us that issues of such moment cannot be safely left to the generals or the economists. Such choices cannot be delegated to the so-called policymakers; they must be discussed by the citizens themselves with reference to the moral guidelines they hold to be valid, realizing that often those guidelines are grounded in religious belief-systems. Any nation that attaches as much importance as America does to what the Founding Fathers called "an active and informed citizenry" should be grateful to the Catholic bishops, not only for the actual statements they made, but for the method they used to prepare them. The bishops circulated drafts of their encyclicals and asked for responses not only from Catholics but from anyone who wished to participate. This whole process reminded large numbers of people that public policy issues are *not* merely technical questions that can be left to experts, but are fundamentally moral and even religious questions that citizens must sort through and argue out with their fellow citizens.

Another positive example of the enlargement of the democratic vista is offered by the American black churches. In recent years they have sought to enlarge and deepen the participation of black people in public policy formation at a mature level. One of the principal vehicles for this effort, although not the only one, has been the presidential candidacy of Jesse Jackson of the Rainbow Coalition. This mode of entry was to be expected. Just as it is understandable that the Roman Catholic community in America should address the larger community through the voice of its collective episcopate, it is also natural that the black community should make a similar move through a particular figure—a black president—who links the black community to the larger society. It is also worth mentioning that many of the positions taken by the Rainbow Coalition draw directly on the prophetic tradition of the Old Testament and on the example of Jesus' preferential ministry to the poor and dispossessed. Thus a genuinely religious perspective is introduced into public policy considerations in a way that cannot be ignored.

But there is also bad news. As usual it comes in "battalions." I see two particular dangers: *trivialization* and *imposition*. One cannot begin to list all the examples of the trivialization of religious influence. It is perhaps worth noting in passing that it would be hard to imagine the impact of Shirley Mac-Laine's curious amalgam of psychic flim-flam, Eastern spirituality, and biblical imagery, were it not for the renewed openness to religious influence that characterizes the whole American scene today. "Remember," Shirley MacLaine tells her followers, "that you are god, so be sure to act that way." In this case "being god" probably does not mean, as it does in the Christian tradition, bearing the sins and sufferings of many. Rather, it means being able to have and be everything anyone wants. It is the ultimate "yuppie" version of religiosity: a religion without discomfort or inconvenience, in which you can have it all.

Shirley MacLaine, however, is only the most consumer-oriented and "user-friendly" example of a much wider religious movement that must be understood to include Jim and Tammy Faye Bakker and the other religious television superstars who appeal to the same mentality she does. The phenomenon of the TV evangelists and of Shirley MacLaine reminds us that a resurgence of religion always brings with it varieties of religion that distort and dilute the traditions from which they spring.

Another grim possibility as a future scenario for the influence of religion in America was suggested by the presidential campaign of Pat Robertson and the support he garnered from other independent TV evangelists such as Jerry Falwell and Jimmy Swaggert. One can of course have no valid complaint about a clergyman running for any public office in America, including that of president. As we have noted, Jesse Jackson has availed himself of this right. What was worrisome about the Robertson campaign, however, was his promise to return us all to a "Christian America." When we hear that phrase, we must remind ourselves first that there has never been (except in pious mythology) a completely Christian America; and, second, that the population of the U.S. today can hardly be adequately described in these terms. In Hawaii, Buddhists hold a near majority. There are now more Jews than Episcopalians in the United States. Jews have been here since the seventeenth century. Indeed, from the earliest years of the republic America has been pluralistic. It included Deists like Benjamin Franklin, Calvinists like George Witherspoon, agnostics like Thomas Jefferson, and conventional Anglicans like George Washington. Our Constitution was written with the maintenance of this pluralism in mind.

But Mr. Robertson has suggested—to the astonishment of some observers—that the Constitutional clause on the nonestablishment of religion that appears in the First Amendment does not apply to the states. It is a remarkable argument. Robertson, a law school graduate, points out that the amendment itself was originally intended as a protection only from *federal* action, and that for years after it was ratified some states (including Massachusetts) continued to have one form or another of established church. As most people will remember, however, in 1868 the U.S. adopted the Fourteenth Amendment, which held that "no State shall make or enforce any law which shall abridge the privileges or immunities of citizens of the U.S." The amendment was intended to apply the Bill of Rights to states as well as to the federal government. Here the issue is joined. Robertson and his supporters believe the Supreme Court was wrong when it banned classroom prayers under the authority of the First Amendment's nonestablishment clause. One way, they believe, to roll back this and similar decisions is to find some way to modify the Establishment Clause itself. Robertson thinks he sees a way. He points out that in 1876, a bill called the Blaine Amendment, which sought to add to the First Amendment the words "... no state shall make any law respecting an establishment of religion ..." failed to get the required two-thirds vote in the Senate. Robertson argues that if the Fourteenth Amendment had been meant to prevent the individual states from establishing or favoring a particular religion, no such proposal would ever have been made. And the fact that the Blaine Amendment failed clearly demonstrates, Robertson contends, that the Senate never intended such an interpretation. Following his logic, the states today should be free of the religious constraints imposed by the First Amendment.

Robertson has not spelled out how his formula would work in detail. Presumably it would allow for a certain state-level "local option" in such matters as school prayer, tax support for private religious schools, teaching creationism, and similar matters. Nor does he explain how he would deal with the fact that the Supreme Court has twice considered the Blaine proposal and found that it does not undermine the Fourteenth Amendment. In a 1985 decision the court said the Fourteenth Amendment had "imposed the same substantive limitations on the States' power to legislate that the First Amendment has always imposed on the Congress' power. This court has confirmed and endorsed this elementary proposition of law time and time again."[3]

Mr. Robertson of course insists that governmental tolerance of religious diversity would continue to be respected under an administration that he would head because God wills such tolerance in the civil realm. But this will not be much comfort for the hundreds of thousands—indeed millions—of Buddhists, Muslims, Jews, and nonbelievers, to say nothing of the many, many Christians who do not agree with his theology. The framing of the Constitution suggests that the maintenance of religious diversity and freedom in America cannot be left to the good intentions of the executive, no matter how closely he is guided by a benevolent deity. It must be written into law and vigorously applied to the courts, and this should happen whether or not those who interpret and apply the law believe they are being guided by God. For the framers of the Constitution, religious liberty was itself a religious value. They believed coercion in matters of faith was an impediment to genuine piety. While he remains a candidate, Robertson's curious views on the First and Fourteenth Amendments can perhaps be dismissed as mere creativity. But as president these views would be downright menacing.

Having now surveyed the global reach, theological significance, and political and moral ambiguity of the resurgence of religion, we are now ready to return to the questions we started with. What is the meaning of the reemergence of religious insti-

3. Tom Teepen, "Pat Robertson and Religious Freedom," *Church and State* 40 (July-August 1987): 17.

tutions and religiously motivated persons into the realm of public policy discourse? Let me say at once that, despite my reservations, I welcome it. I do not share the fear of those people who believe that this reentry will inevitably destroy the fragile fabric of our political and religious pluralism. I do not agree that religion must be consigned to the private realm and that all public discourse must be purged of religious reference, though I do not think quoting the popes or the Bible is the best *strategy* in the public realm. We have come through a period in American history in which some people have tried to create a form of public policy discourse that advertises itself as free of value judgments and religious biases, a management science in which expertise is what counts. But public policy is not merely a matter of the expert manipulation of institutions and practices. It is ultimately a matter of moral debate. Politics without morality is reduced to a kind of plumbing. Morality without politics inevitably becomes trivial and exotic. But politics and morality must be joined in a way that enables all parties to speak and be heard and to make decisions based on the kind of moral consensus that can emerge only when the moral bases for policy choices are made explicit. Richard P. McBrien uses the term "public church" to characterize this public side of religious participation in American democracy. "Unlike the fundamentalists," McBrien says, "with their talk of a 'Christian nation,' or the individualists, lost in their own world of consumer religion, adherents of the public church are committed to and care about the principle of religious liberty and the cultivation of religious pluralism."[4]

The key word here is *cultivation.* Real religious pluralism is not just something we must tolerate. We must *nurture* it. One reason we must do so is that as these moral bases of policy choices are made explicit, we will inevitably find ourselves in a more *explicitly* pluralistic religious world. I hope this will not deter us. But it will make us rethink our school system and the way we prepare our children to take part in public discourse.

4. Richard P. McBrien, *Caesar's Coin: Religion and Politics in America* (New York: Macmillan, 1987).

This is where "cultivation" is called for. The time is past when we could pretend that the schools could be insulated from the religious and moral pluralism of our heterogeneous society. The challenge now is not to keep the schools free of any such influence but to find ways to introduce these various perspectives in a responsible and interesting manner. What we need is not a return to officially sanctioned prayer in the public schools, but a curriculum that helps children learn how to live in a religiously plural society.

The question of just how much influence religion has had, now has, or will have on American society is at best only a preliminary one. The question is really not so much a quantitative one—how much?—but a qualitative one—how? *How* can those of us who are religious in one way and those of us who are religious in another listen to and speak to each other, so that our differences and our diversity become strengths we can draw on to build a more genuinely pluralistic society? *How* can we help each other recognize both the strength and the fragility of the religious pluralism we have accomplished in the United States and the valuable gift that pluralism represents for the tasks we must undertake in the future? These are the real "how's" we need to address.

Epilogue:
Speculations and Conclusions

Albright G. Zimmerman

In this concluding chapter, rather than summarizing the foregoing chapters an ambitious attempt will be made to identify and clarify the often cloudy issues of religion and society that face our republic. Following a brief discussion of the constitutional legacy inherited from the Founding Fathers and from the nineteenth-century leaders of our nation, we will consider many of the changes wrought in our society during the last two hundred years. Then I will try to trace the often debatable chronological development of the Supreme Court's positions and interpretations of the various issues that are of such major concern today. I hope to spell these out with some clarity, although complete objectivity is obviously impossible. The focus will be on those particular areas where the courts have failed to come to meaningful and universally satisfying conclusions. Finally, the positions of critics from the various political and ideological spectrums will be evaluated, and we will conclude with some general either/or speculations as to what may lie ahead in this unsettled arena.

In the Constitution itself only one statement is specifically concerned with religion, a clause that states that "no religious test shall ever be required as a qualification to any office or trust under the United States."[1] Then in the First Amendment one finds the provision that "Congress shall make no law respecting an establishment of religion, or prohibiting the free exercise thereof." However, it is the Fourteenth Amendment (adopted 1868), specifically in its first and fifth sections, that is the basis for the most bitter constitutional disputes. These sections read as follows:

> Section 1: All persons born or naturalized in the United States, and subject to the jurisdiction thereof, are citizens of the United States and of the State wherein they reside. No State shall . . . abridge the privileges or immunities of citizens of the United States; nor shall any State deprive any person of life, liberty, or property, without due process of law; nor deny to any person within its jurisdiction the equal protection of the laws.

> Section 5: The Congress shall have the power to enforce, by appropriate legislation, the provisions of this article.

These statements combine to shape the relationship of church and state that is debated today.

I. The Founders—Architects of What?

The Founding Fathers, children of the Enlightenment and in most cases individuals experienced in the duties of government, conceptualized the goals of the Constitutional Convention in realistic terms. They created a new federal establishment and delegated to it specific and limited powers—but powers sufficient to eliminate the inadequacies in the Articles of Confederation. At the same time, by permitting the states to retain all other powers, the founders satisfied a variety of local concerns that were probably held by a majority of the American people. By basing the authority for establishing the new government on the

---

1. Constitution of the United States, Art. VII, Sec. 3.

general populace, they recognized the people as the prime basis of sovereignty. They created a lower house based on popular electorates with the states determining the qualifications of electors. The opening lines of the Constitution's Preamble, "We the people of the United States . . . do ordain and establish this Constitution," illustrates their recognition that the document would be based on the people. They then arranged for the existing state governments to be bypassed in the ratification procedures with a provision that the ratification should be by special conventions in each of the states and not by legislatures. The Constitution was written primarily in the negative and contained specific guarantees *against* any possible impositions on the rights and freedoms of individuals by the new government and allowed the states or the people to retain all powers not specifically delegated to the new federal government. One should remember, writes Michael Kammen, that "the founders did not expect their instrument of government to achieve utopia: merely national stability, economic growth and individual liberty."[2] The Constitution was not the idealized, symmetrical construct of the political philosopher but rather the product of pragmatic men, practiced in the art of government, who by necessity recognized the existence of the thirteen existing states and incorporated them into the new constitutional system.

There was general recognition of ground rules that limited national authority except where specifically noted, particularly those specified in the Bill of Rights, which was proposed in Congress in 1789 and finally adopted and put into effect under the new national government on December 15, 1791. In 1833 Chief Justice John Marshall, in his *Barron* v. *Baltimore* decision,[3] established the supremacy of the Constitution and implemented the authority of the federal courts in the area of judicial review. He carefully observed the parameters set in the original Constitution by the Founding Fathers when he ruled that the Bill of

2. Michael Kammen, *A Machine That Would Go of Itself: The Constitution in American Culture* (New York: Alfred A. Knopf, 1986), p. 398.
3. 7 Pet. 243 (1833).

Rights applied only against the federal government and not against the states.

John F. Wilson in a perceptive review of two important recent books, Thomas J. Curry's study of church and state relations in early America and Leonard W. Levy's study of the Establishment Clause, notes that both authors left out "the middle ground," the period between our present and the "remote past" of the Founding Fathers. This may not be completely true in the case of Levy, who is an unrestrained and often emotional supporter of absolute separation, as he makes a less than judicious analysis of the Fourteenth Amendment and the incorporation of the First Amendment into the Fourteenth.[4]

II. Changes over Time

At this point we need to take note of some of the changes that have occurred in the past two hundred years. During that period, the population grew from the nearly 4 million recorded in the first decennial census of 1790 to a number that is approaching 250 million in 1989. A predominately agrarian society in 1790 (95 percent rural), the country changed until the 1890 census revealed that for the first time the urban population exceeded the rural—a trend that has continued until today when more than 77 percent of the population is classified as urban (and this percentage is undervalued as a result of changes in the statistical methodology used by the Census Bureau).[5] From a relatively poor

4. John F. Wilson, review of Thomas J. Curry, *The First Freedoms: Church and State in America to the Passage of the First Amendment* (New York: Oxford Univ. Press, 1986), and review of Leonard W. Levy, *The Establishment Clause: Religion and the First Amendment* (New York: Macmillan, 1986), in *Reviews in American History* 15 (Dec. 1987): 585-90.

5. U.S. Census Bureau, *Historical Statistics of the United States: Colonial Times to 1970* (Washington: U.S. Government Printing Office, 1975), Series A-57-72, "Population in Urban and Rural Territory by Size of Place, 1790–1970"; U.S. Census Bureau, *National Data Book and Guide to Sources, Statistical Abstract of the United States*, 108th ed. (Washington, D.C.: U.S. Government Printing Office, 1977), Table No. 30; see also Wade Clark Roof, "Denominational Amer-

country in 1790, a debtor nation with relatively few accumulations of capital, the nation grew until by the end of World War II, it was, at least monetarily, the richest nation in the world and a creditor nation. In recent years, suffering from a negative balance of trade and constantly-rising consumer consumption, at least partly the result of a revolution in aspirations, many question the overall economic health of the country, even in the face of a growth in the economy characterized by increasing national product and reduced unemployment. A country that in 1790 was 95 percent Christian, predominately Protestant (although this did not correlate with formal church membership), now has a far more heterogeneous makeup, Protestants collectively constituting at best little more than a slight majority as the Catholic and Orthodox communicants along with Jews now approach the number of Protestants. The pluralistic mix of the national population has been further complicated by the arrival of growing numbers of often non-Christian Asiatics and Africans, many of whom are professed Muslims, Buddhists, or some other variety of religious persuasion exotic to the American tradition. In addition to a growing number of publicly professed atheists, one finds adherents to proselytizing religions, popularly referred to as cults, such as the Unification Church and Hare Krishna, that are rapidly growing as a result of conversions among the existing American populace. Ideologically, the traditional value structures based on the Judeo-Christian tradition are faced with competition in the public arena from competing mass so-called democratic movements that range from welfare-minority movements to a variety of Marxist and Freudian Humanist programs. In addition to providing a previously undreamed of plenitude of material goods, a scientific-technological revolution has also provided explanations both for natural phenomena and for human maladies, thus encroaching on the earlier theological preserve of explaining irrational and mysterious life crises.

---

ica and the New Religious Pluralism," *Annals of the American Academy of Political and Social Science* 480 (July 1985): 24-38, reprinted in *Religion in American Life,* ed. Janet Podell (New York: H. W. Wilson, 1987), pp. 9-26.

It is impossible to overestimate the impact on the fabric of American society of the approximately thirty-five million people who came to America between 1870 and 1914 as part of the "New Immigration," most of whom came from cultural heritages that differed appreciably from that of a predominately Protestant Christian America. At least equal consideration should be given to what could be called the "New New Immigration" of the period from 1945 to the present, whose legal and illegal components possibly number in the tens of millions. These people come from even more alien cultures, often non-Christian, and with nontraditional political and ideological beliefs and life-styles that are disturbing to many Americans. They are sometimes incredibly poor, but often they come with appreciable financial resources, creating foreign language enclaves, particularly in the cities but also in suburbia, where they demand bilingual education and where they create communities in which Spanish or some other language is replacing English.[6]

In the process, they continue to question, as did the earlier immigrants, what Robert Handy has referred to as the "validity of Christian Morals." What is the distinction between a Christian Nation, a Christian nation with a church militant, and a moral nation? Sanford Levinson in his new work, *Constitutional Faith*, argues that there are distinctively "Protestant" and "Catholic" approaches to interpretations of the Constitution. According to Lucas A. Powe, Jr., in his review of Levinson's work, the "Protestant" constitutionalist treats the "Constitution-as-text and criticizes the institutional claims of the Supreme Court to give 'final' interpretations of the text." On the other hand, the "'Catholic' constitutionalists . . . stress the 'unwritten' components . . . that coexist with the . . . 'written' text," and also accept "the supremacy of the Supreme Court." According to Powe, Levinson's

---

6. For a specific case, see Nicholas Lemann, "Growing Pains," *The Atlantic,* January 1988, pp. 57-62; also Charles Lockwood and Christopher B. Leinberger, "Los Angeles Comes of Age," *The Atlantic,* January 1988, pp. 31-56, particularly the section entitled "America's First 'Third World City,'" pp. 41-44. For a broader perspective, see the special issue of *Time* magazine on immigrants, 8 July 1985, pp. 24-101.

work helps to explain the lines drawn in the Bork hearings. It is interesting that Levinson also calls upon the Pharisee-Sadducee analogy used by Max Stackhouse in an earlier version of his paper found in this volume. These distinctions are perceptive, but I believe that in many areas the Protestant and Catholic categories somewhat beg reality. For example, in the patterns of support for nonpublic schools, Levinson's judgment may be on target, but in other areas such as law and order the application has some problems and the distinctions may be suspect.[7]

Many of the later-nineteenth-century "New Immigrants" came to America with no idea of becoming permanent residents, certainly not with the idea of becoming "Americans," and definitely not in the Protestant mold. Recent research has revealed that many came only to improve themselves financially and had every intention of taking their gains and returning to their country of origin. Interestingly, however, many who did return to their former homeland did not stay but returned to a country that now had attractions for them.[8]

We can exaggerate divergence but we can also overvalue unifying forces. In Federalist No. 10 we find the primary documentation for Madison's assumption that diversity in the face of great size provided "pluralistic" guarantees against tyranny. Technology has enhanced communications and has broken down traditional communities. One might ask, however, if the media with its sophisticated instruments of mass communication in a world of material plenty and high technology has

7. Sanford Levinson, *Constitutional Faith* (Princeton: Princeton Univ. Press, 1988), pp. 18-53; review by Lucas A. Powe, Jr., in *The History Book Club Review,* Sept. 1988, pp. 16-17.

8. E.g., Humbert S. Nelli, *From Immigrants to Ethnics: The Italian Americans* (New York: Oxford Univ. Press, 1983), esp. pp. 42ff.; also William I. Thomas and Florian Znaniecki, *The Polish Peasant in Europe and America,* 2d ed. (New York: Dover Publications, 1958), 2:1492-1503; Frank J. Coppa, "Those Who Followed Columbus: The Italian Migration to the United States of America," in *The Immigrant Experience in America,* ed. Thomas J. Curran and Frank J. Coppa (Boston: Twayne Publishers, 1976), pp. 115-46, 120; Timothy L. Smith, "Immigrant Social Aspirations in American Education, 1880–1930," *American Quarterly* 21 (1969): 523-43.

changed the rules of the game as expressed by Madison's Federalist No. 10. Has the demagoguery, so feared in smaller communities by the Founding Fathers, become a reality on a national scale through the instrumentality of the electronic media?[9]

Were the Founding Fathers who authored the Constitution with its "no test" provisions and its non-Establishment clause somehow transferred to the modern world, they would probably be stunned by our age's preoccupation with school prayer, support for public versus nonpublic education, debates on abortion and right to life, along with the secular libertarian and pluralistic demands for "rights." They would probably judge themselves to be in a lunatic asylum. To them, the pleas of social libertarians or any of their ilk for permissiveness would be an anathema. Although Jefferson authored the metaphoric wall of separation between church and state, neither he nor any of his contemporaries saw this as a barrier denying civil authority the power to police morals, let alone as an invitation for secular license and excess. In fact, if we recall that the age still supported sumptuary laws that regulated excessiveness of dress, particularly for the ordinary classes, we may comprehend some sense of the degree of approval generally held for the secular control of social morality, a social morality that was generally based on scriptural authority.[10]

Theirs was the world of the Enlightenment, a world that recognized "reason" or authority hallowed by tradition or perhaps revelation—but a revelation that must be based on venerable age. Their view was of a man-centered stage on which was worked out the comic and tragic scenario of human existence. An idealized prototype of the Enlightenment would be an in-

---

9. Neil Riemer, *James Madison* (New York: Washington Square Press, 1968), pp. 36-39, 126-27, 187-88.

10. See Gordon S. Wood, *The Creation of the American Republic, 1776–1787* (Chapel Hill: Univ. of North Carolina Press, 1969), pp. 64-65, 110-11; for specific laws in the early years of the Massachusetts Bay Colony, see Richard B. Morris, *Government and Labor in Early America* (1946; rpt., New York: Harper Torchbooks, 1965), p. 69; concerning ostentatious dress for apprentices and servants see pp. 383-84.

dividual who had experienced victory as his rational faculties won out over his base passions in the internal and, yes, eternal struggle that was taking place in every moral person. In the process of developing these internal faculties, he became aware of immutable and moral natural law that predicated a social and moral creature with a republican Roman's commitment to duty and service. It was a stage on which a single plot was acted and reenacted over and over again, the story of man's attempt to conquer his baser nature, whether the story was orchestrated in Enlightenment terms or in theistic providential terms.

In contrast, we live in a world where the human center stage disappeared as Charles Darwin and Charles Lyell "proved" an evolution that substituted accident, probability, and change over the ages for providential and theocratic explanations. Instead of a single human-based scenario, today we have a myriad of adventitious dramas seemingly with little direction and much drift. Reason and moral faculties have been replaced by the irrationality of the romantic reaction and subsequently have been given a final *coup de grace* by the subconscious and myth of Sigmund Freud. In the physical world reason has paled in the face of Werner Heisenberg's theory of indeterminacy and the almost nihilistic attacks on any metaphysical explanation by the logical positivists, who deny any truths that cannot be reduced to mathematical formulation, and finally by the relativism and situational ethics of the existentialists.[11]

Throughout most of the nineteenth century the mainstream—or perhaps we should say the power structure—operated as if America were a Protestant nation, despite the growing numbers of non-Protestants, and schools moved into the twentieth century with required Bible readings (from the King James Version), compulsory recitation of the Lord's Prayer,

11. For at least some consideration of the impact of evolution see John C. Greene, *The Death of Adam: Evolution and Its Impact on Western Thought* (Ames: Iowa State Univ. Press, 1959), *passim;* see also Peter J. Bowler, *Evolution: The History of an Idea* (Berkeley and Los Angeles: Univ. of California Press, 1984), chaps. 8 and 12.

and a curriculum where the "patrician" traditions in literature and historical interpretation were *de rigour*.[12] It was not until the twentieth century, after World War II, according to Robert T. Handy, that concern for civil rights and the rights of ethnic, racial, and gender groups started to change this orientation, aided by a new "activist" Supreme Court. Only then did what has become the ideal for many, the pluralistic society, truly come into existence.[13] We should also direct our attention to the Progressive period when the new history produced by Charles A. Beard and Vernon L. Parrington, among others, exposed a past history that told a story of privilege and poverty, exploitation and injustice, instead of one of opportunity and greatness.[14]

III. The Issues

One of the most challenging questions to be addressed as we try to get a handle on today's church-state problems is, have the ground rules of the relationship been altered? Certainly the parameters have been. When the Constitution was written and the new government instituted, secular versus religious education was not an issue. The idea of a free public school, supported by taxes, did not become a reality until bitter legislative battles were fought in Pennsylvania where two unlikely partisans, the Jacksonian Democrat Governor George Wolfe and the anti-Masonic Whig partisan Thaddeus Stevens united in support of the concept of universal free education. Prior to this time, the Northwest Land Ordinance of 1785 provided that section number 16 of the public lands should go to support public education, yet the initiation and supervision of the school was often delegated

12. See *School District of Abington* v. *Schempp*, 374 U.S. 203 (1963); Richard Hofstadter, *The Progressive Historians: Turner, Beard and Parrington* (New York: Alfred A. Knopf, 1968), chap. 1, "Background."

13. See Robert T. Handy's essay in this volume.

14. E.g., Hofstadter, *Progressive Historians, passim;* also John Higham with Leonard Krieger and Felix Gilbert, *History* (Englewood Cliffs, N.J.: Prentice Hall, 1964), Part III, esp. pp. 171-232.

to a religious body and the costs incurred were usually assessed against the families of the school children; inability to pay the "fair share" resulted in the necessity of signing the demeaning pauper's oath.[15] We should note, however, that the question of fairness in the delivery of a quality educational opportunity to all segments of the population is still an open issue.

Likewise, the question of prayer in the schools rarely if ever came into consideration until the nineteenth century, when large numbers of German and Irish immigrants created the first real "ghettos" in urban centers where they often attempted to retain their identity through religiously oriented foreign language schools. It is largely forgotten or ignored that in the early nineteenth century, tax money did occasionally support church schools, and many prominent Americans including New York Governor William H. Seward seriously supported the concept of publicly supported church schools. Lawrence A. Cremin, in his magisterial history of American education, describes these far from simple debates and decisions in some detail, although he unfortunately ignores Pennsylvania's struggles for the free common school. Lutherans, Presbyterians, and many other groups tried to get part of the public largess, and it is interesting to note that it was following defeats in the New York legislature that Roman Catholic Bishop John Hughes pronounced, "let us then leave the public schools to themselves," as he called upon Catholics to set out and create a church-supported Catholic school system.[16]

The Civil War saw a tremendous expansion in the exercise of national authority that resulted in a dominance by the federal

15. Philip S. Klein and Ari Hoogenboom, *A History of Pennsylvania,* 2d ed. (University Park: Pennsylvania State Univ. Press, 1980), pp. 145-46; "Reports of the Philadelphia Public Schools, 1819–1850," in *Sources of the American Social Tradition,* vol. 1, ed. David J. Rothman and Sheila Rothman (New York: Basic Books, 1975), pp. 172-77; Frank Tracy Carlton, *Economic Influences Upon Educational Progress in the United States, 1820–1850* (New York: Teachers College Press, 1966).

16. Lawrence A. Cremin, *American Education: The National Experience, 1783–1896* (San Francisco: Harper & Row, 1980), chap. 5, "Systems of Schooling," pp. 148-85; quote is from pp. 168-69.

government. During the Reconstruction period, an aggressive Congress that seemingly was implementing its dominance over the executive branch imposed the authority of the national government over the southern states with the constitutionally questionable Civil Rights Acts. These acts were subsequently validated with the ratification of three constitutional amendments. The Fourteenth, the most important of the three, at least guaranteed the new freedman's basic civil rights against both the states and the federal government. While it seems that this was all that the authors of the amendment intended, its purpose has been debated since that time. In fact, the intensity of the arguments has increased, particularly since the 1920s. Over time, the Fourteenth Amendment has been used to alter the parameters of constitutionalism to a greater degree than has any other amendment to the Constitution. The interpretation of the Constitution through the decisions of the courts, particularly of the Supreme Court since the passage of the Fourteenth Amendment, constitutes the essence of the unsettled arena. Until the 1950s, the civil rights of the freed slave and his black descendants were essentially ignored and most legal arguments turned on questions of what the terms *due process* and *equal protection* in the first section of the amendment meant, especially in the areas of free speech and freedom of the press.

IV. The Role of the Court

In this section I will attempt to provide an overview of the direction of the Court insofar as its decisions are perceived to affect religion and religious freedom. In many cases, these considerations go well beyond the clauses of the First Amendment. For example, the constitutional "right to privacy" on which the abortion decisions are primarily based is rooted in the Fourth Amendment, which deals with questions of freedom from search and seizure. From 1868 into the 1920s—through the Slaughterhouse Cases and the unsuccessful Blaine Amendment and into the prosperity decade of the 1920s—the rule of the

Court seems to have been judicial restraint and a devotion to ordered liberty.[17]

In 1922, the Supreme Court in *Prudential Insurance Co.* v. *Cheek* ruled that "neither the Fourteenth Amendment nor any other provisions of the Constitution of the United States imposes upon the States any restriction about 'freedom of speech.'"[18]

According to most of the commentators, the pattern started to change in 1925 in *Gitlow* v. *New York*,[19] a case in which the Supreme Court stated its assumption "that freedom of speech and the press . . . are among the fundamental personal rights and 'liberties' protected by the due process clause of the 14th amendment from impairment by the States."[20] Justice San-

---

17. For the development of the concept of "ordered liberty," see Michael Kammen, *Spheres of Liberty: Changing Perceptions of Liberty in American Culture* (Madison: Univ. of Wisconsin Press, 1986), and Archibald Cox, *The Court and the Constitution* (Boston: Houghton Mifflin, 1987). The selectivity of the various so-called authorities concerning the Blaine Amendment is interesting. Leo Pfeffer takes note of the amendment, yet Levy ignores it, while several of the accomodationists, particularly James McClelland, place great weight on the debates over the amendment and particularly the language of individuals who also had significant roles in the introduction and passage of the Fourteenth Amendment. Pfeffer gets an entirely different reading from the same debates; see Leo Pfeffer, *Church, State and Freedom*, rev. ed. (Boston: Beacon Press, 1967), pp. 146-47; Levy, *Establishment Clause*, pp. 165-68, and "The Establishment Clause," in *How Does the Constitution Protect Religious Freedom?* ed. Robert A. Goldwin and Art Kaufman (Washington, D.C.: American Enterprise Institute for Public Policy Research, 1988), pp. 85-87; James McClelland, "Hand's Writing on the Wall of Separation: The Significance of *Jaffree* in Future Cases on Religious Establishment," in Goldwin and Kaufman, pp. 43-68.

18. 259 U.S. 530, 543 (1922); quoted in Cox, *Court and Constitution*, p. 190.

19. 268 U.S. 652.

20. 286 U.S. 652 (1925), quoted in Edward S. Corwin, *Liberty Against Government: The Rise, Flowering and Decline of a Famous Judicial Concept* (Baton Rouge: Louisiana State Univ. Press, 1948), p. 155; the Court had already in *Meyer* v. *Nebraska* (262 U.S. 380) set aside state statutes forbidding the teaching of foreign languages in the first eight grades. In 1925 in *Pierce* v. *Society of Sisters* (268 U.S. 510), a state law that outlawed other than state schools was overturned. Religion was involved here, for the decision prevented the state from outlawing what in this case were specifically religious schools. *Pierce* was cited in *Zorach* v. *Clauson* (343 U.S. 306 [1952]) and in *School District of Abington* v. *Schempp* (374 U.S. 303 [1968]); see Francis Graham Lee, *Wall of Controversy: Church-State Conflict in America, the Justices and Their Opinions* (Melbourne, Fla.: Robert E. Krieger, 1986), pp. 34, 36, 44.

ford, who included the foregoing statement in his majority decision, offered no citations to justify the assumption, something that is pointedly noted by the accomodationists and by most proponents of original intent, along with two major constitutional historians, Charles Warren and Edward S. Corwin. Corwin would become almost paranoid against what he saw as an unjustified judicial seizure of power.[21]

This undocumented precedent now became the basis for further expansions of the jurisdiction of the Fourteenth Amendment. In the dissent in the same case, Justice Oliver Wendell Holmes, Jr., supported by Justice Louis D. Brandais, stated the doctrine of "clear and present danger," which subsequently provided a rationale for federal intervention in free speech cases.[22] In 1931, in the seldom cited case of *Near* v. *Minnesota*,[23] the Supreme Court overturned a state law and the decisions of two lower federal courts and established the principle that freedom of the press was incorporated into the Fourteenth Amendment.[24]

In 1937, in *Palko* v. *Connecticut*,[25] Justice Benjamin N. Cardozo had this to say concerning freedom of thought and speech:

> One may say that it is the matrix, the indispensable condition of nearly every form of freedom. . . . So it has come about that the domain of liberty, withdrawn by the Fourteenth Amendment from encroachment by the states, has been enlarged by latter-day judgements to include liberty of the mind as well as liberty of action. The extension became, indeed, a logical imperative when once it was recognized, as long ago it was, that liberty is something more than exemption from physical restraints, and that even in the field of substantive rights and duties the legislative judgement, if oppressive and arbitrary, may be overridden by the courts.

21. See Corwin, *Liberty Against Government.*
22. Corwin, *Liberty Against Government*, pp. 155-56; McClelland, "Hand's Writing," p. 50; Levy, "Establishment Clause," p. 86.
23. 283 U.S. 697.
24. McClelland, "Hand's Writing," p. 51.
25. 302 U.S. 319, and 327.

According to Archibald Cox, Cardozo's approach suggested "selective incorporation of those Bill of Rights guarantees which were 'of the very essence of a scheme for ordered liberty' but it would neither incorporate all the guarantees nor bar" a selective application to the first ten amendments.[26]

The various commentators seem to be in agreement that Justice Hugo L. Black delivered the final *coup de grace* in his majority opinion in the case of *Everson* v. *Board of Education* as he pronounced that "the First Amendment . . . as made applicable to the States by the Fourteenth . . . commands that a state . . . make no law" establishing or prohibiting free exercise. He ruled that the bus service under question for parochial school students constituted service for the students and not for religion and did not create a breech in "the wall between church and state. That wall," he continued, "must be kept high and impregnable."[27]

To Leo Pfeffer and the other absolute separationists, the foregoing debates were, at least intellectually, an exercise in futility. For them the First Amendment to the Constitution had called for an absolute separation of church and state, a separation symbolized by Jefferson's metaphorical "wall." Further, the Fourteenth Amendment had meant just what it said—it applied equal protection and due process against the states. To the separationists, there's no room for any argument. There can be no material support of any kind to private or religious schools nor religious instruction of any kind in secular schools or in public buildings, and at least by today's interpretations there should be an almost absolute freedom for the individual even in areas such as sex and conception and as well in matters of free speech, free press, and life-styles, however deviant. Additionally, the separationists question the constitutionality of tax exemption for religious institutions and would like to guarantee free exercise to almost any variety of variant religion or cult and protect

26. Quoted in Corwin, *Liberty Against Government,* pp. 156-57; Cox, *Court and Constitution,* p. 241.

27. *Everson* v. *Board of Education,* 330 U.S. 1 (1947); Cox, *Court and Constitution,* pp. 241-42; see also *Adamson* v. *California,* 332 U.S. 46 (1947).

the widest range of free speech or other expression.[28] The American Civil Liberties Union (ACLU) generally supports all of these positions although the organization occasionally clouds its repute as a "liberal" organization by opposing a perceived violation of a civil right on behalf of a conservative, sometimes even a despised reactionary or an unpopular religious cult.[29]

The accomodationists, committed to what they sometimes called "a government neutrality theory," consist largely but not exclusively of Roman Catholic supporters of parochial schools who interpret the Constitution to mean that it is constitutional, in the words of Henry J. Abraham, to transform

> a religious school classroom into a "public" one by hanging a sign "public school" on the outside of that classroom to circumvent strictures against excessive church-state entanglements or compelling public school children of minority religions to recite prayers from the New Testament.[30]

Generally the fundamentalists, particularly Baptists, oppose the accomodationists on the support for parochial education issue, but align themselves with the accomodationists on school prayer, release time, tax exemption, and public religious observances. The fundamentalist movement, according to not necessarily friendly commentators, is in

28. See Leo Pfeffer's essay in this volume; also Richard John Neuhaus, "The Pfefferian Inversion," *National Review,* 13 May 1988, p. 44. Robert L. Cord, *Separation of Church and State: Historical Fact and Current Fiction* (New York: Lambeth Press, 1982), is a running commentary attempting to refute Pfeffer.

29. E.g., see Richard E. Morgan, *Disabling America: The "Rights Industry" in Our Time* (New York: Basic Books, 1984), pp. 204-7; for a detailed example of the ACLU defending an unpopular position, see James L. Gibson and Richard D. Bingham, *Civil Liberties and Nazis: The Skokie Free-Speech Controversy* (New York: Praeger, 1985), cvm.

30. Henry J. Abraham, "Religion, the Constitution, the Court, and Society: Some Contemporary Reflections on Mandates, Words, Human Beings, and the Art of the Possible," in *How Does the Constitution . . . ,* ed. Goldwin and Kaufman, pp. 15-42, quote on p. 16; for a thoughtful discussion of theories of "neutrality," see Carl H. Esbeck, "Religion and a Neutral State: Imperative or Impossibility?" *Vital Speeches of the Day* 50 (1 July 1984): 548-55, reprinted in *Religion in American Life,* ed. Podell, pp. 146-51.

the revivalist tradition [which] is socially diverse and culturally paradoxical. . . . It is torn between controversial and uncivil rejection of unbelievers in a pluralistic society and their warm embrace to help win souls for Christ. It actively engages larger public issues to help redeem the city of the world, and it forsakes a sinful world to seek the City of God. This ambiguity reflects Fundamentalists' sense of being outsiders in the twentieth century, a scorned minority in secular America.[31]

According to George M. Marsden, fundamentalists are committed to a folklore that is

a popularization of a version of the Whig view of history, in which true religion and liberty are always pitted against false religion and tyranny. America, in this view, was founded on Christian principles embodied in the Constitution and has been chosen by God to be a beacon of right religion and liberty for the whole world.[32]

Today's Supreme Court, according to many critics, has consistently moved beyond constitutionally justifiable positions. From a posture generally labeled "judicial restraint," which had been the stance of the Supreme Court in the 1930s, the judiciary gave indications of significant changes in this attitude during and after World War II. During the subsequent years, the Court finally incorporated the Bill of Rights into the Fourteenth Amendment and by using the Equal Protection and the Due Process clauses of that amendment has altered its posture from judicial restraint to one that recognizes the "suspect classifications" and "invidious distinctions" that require "strictest judicial scrutiny."

31. In *Individualism and Commitment in American Life: Readings on the Themes of Habits of the Heart,* ed. Robert N. Bellah, Richard Madsen, William M. Sullivan, Ann Swidler, and Steven M. Tipton (San Francisco: Harper & Row, 1987), p. 324.

32. George M. Marsden, "Preachers of Paradox," in *Individualism and Commitment,* ed. Bellah et al., pp. 336-47, quote on p. 339; see also Gerard V. Bradley, *Church-State Relationships in America* (Westport, Conn: Greenwood Press, 1987), p. 141; for a sympathetic treatment, see Richard John Neuhaus, "What the Fundamentalists Want," *Commentary,* May 1985, pp. 41-46, reprinted in *Religion in American Life,* ed. Podell, pp. 222-35.

The Warren Court (1953–1969) extrapolated a "new Equal Protection Clause" and gave the new dimensions of "Liberty" that enabled the federal courts to overturn state provisions in the areas of voting rights, racial discrimination, economic equality, and then sex (which subsequently was expanded into "gender"). In the process they discovered that the "Liberty" that was distilled out of the new Equal Protection Clause included the constitutional "right to privacy." According to Archibald Cox, solicitor of the United States under Nixon and sometime hero of the Democratic left when he resigned from that administration during the so-called Saturday Night Massacre, nothing in the original Constitution guarantees equality, let alone privacy.[33] In the process, the Court has alienated many Americans by usurping control of voting rights from the states, by "legislating" economic guarantees for the economically deprived, by dictating school busing, and finally, by using the "right to privacy" to protect the criminal and to make sexual equality a prime subject for "strictest judicial scrutiny." As a result the legacy of the Court has been confusion and contradiction.

In the arena of government aid to church-related schools, Justice Hugo Black in *Everson* v. *Board of Education,*[34] as has already been noted, pronounced that it was appropriate to use public monies to pay for busing parochial school students. In 1968, the Court reaffirmed the constitutionality of loaning secular school books to students in religious schools, which previously had been sustained in a 1930s case.[35] And in 1970, in *Walz* v. *Tax Commission,* a case challenging the tax exemption for religious institutions, the Court added a new criteria to sustain the whole tax exemption concept. Added to the two already established tests—that the activity must have a "secular purpose" and that its principal and primary purpose must

33. Cox, *Court and Constitution,* pp. 251-52.

34. 330 U.S. 1 (1947).

35. *Cochran* v. *Louisiana State Board of Education,* 261 U.S. 370 (1930); *Board of Education* v. *Allen,* 392 U.S. 236 (1968).

neither advance nor inhibit religion[36]—is the principle of "excessive entanglement," which is to be avoided by the courts.

In 1971, the Court outlawed contracts that had been entered into by the states to compensate parochial schools for the instruction they furnished their pupils in secular subjects. The rationale was to avoid "excessive entanglements."[37] On June 25, 1973, the Supreme Court handed down a number of decisions: they ruled against a New York law that provided for direct monetary payments to schools serving communities with high concentrations of low-income families and against a similar Pennsylvania plan for tuition reimbursement. On the same day they ruled against any compensation to parochial schools for the preparation and administration of state-mandated but partially internally prepared batteries of tests.[38] In 1974 in *Wheeler* v. *Barrera*[39] the Court ruled that states receiving funds under Title I of the Elementary and Secondary Act must provide "comparable but not identical" services in both public and private schools, even where this would be in conflict with state law, or the state should forfeit such funds. In 1975, the Court struck down all portions of a Pennsylvania bill except the portion calling for the loan of secular textbooks to religious schools. It was ruled that audio-visual equipment and "materials"—periodicals, photographs, maps, and films—could advance religious teachings while "auxiliary services"—remedial teaching, psychological and therapeutic services, guidance counseling, and testing by state-paid personnel—would involve "excessive entanglement."[40] In 1977 an Ohio law sustained legislation that in addition to the lending of textbooks permitted state-financed academic testing using standard tests and state-subsidized

36. Now called the Lemon Test; see *Lemon* v. *Kurtzman,* 403 U.S. 602 (1971); also Cox, *Court and Constitution,* pp. 203, 207-8.

37. *Early* v. *DiCenso,* 403 U.S. 602 (1971); *Lemon* v. *Kurtzman.*

38. *Committee for Public Education and Religious Liberty (PEARL)* v. *Nyquist,* 413 U.S. 756 (1973); *Sloan* v. *Lemon,* 413 U.S. 825 (1973); *Levitt* v. *Committee for Public Education and Religious Liberty (PEARL)* ,413 U.S. 472 (1973).

39. 417 U.S. 664 (1970).

40. *Meek* v. *Pittenger,* 421 U.S. 349 (1975).

speech, hearing, and psychological tests to be administered in the parochial schools by public school employees.[41] In 1983 the Court considered a Minnesota case, *Mueler* v. *Allen,*[42] that permitted state tax deductions from reported gross income for expenses incurred for "tuition, textbooks or transportation." The act was sustained, the rationale basically being that the benefits, at least as legislated, indicated no preference for religious schools.[43]

In the summer of 1988, the Supreme Court sustained the 1981 Adolescent Family Life Act, sometimes known as the Chastity Act, by a 5-4 vote. This act provided federal funds to private, including religious, groups for teen-pregnancy prevention programs that seek alternatives to abortion such as sexual abstinence or adoption. No money was provided for family-planning and abortion programs.[44] The contradictions implicit in the foregoing can only lead to speculation about the future, particularly as many of the decisions were by a 5-4 division and, because of prospective retirements, the makeup of the court is in the process of change. By 1982, only three out of the fifty states failed to offer publicly funded services in some manner to religious schools. Twenty-six states had textbook loar.s; twenty-seven offered bus services; twenty-three furnished health services; twenty-eight supported release time; seventeen subsidized administrative services (testing and record-keeping); fifteen provided special education subsidies; four offered driver education; and two gave tax deductions for special educational expenses.[45]

Chief Justice Rehnquist, in his *Wallace* v. *Jaffree* dissent, listed some of the contradictions in the realm of aid to parochial schools. For example:

41. *Wolman* v. *Walter,* 433 U.S. 229 (1977).

42. Slip no. 82-195 U.S. 9 (1983).

43. For a detailed analysis, see Leo Pfeffer, *Religion, State and the Burger Court* (Buffalo: Prometheus Books, 1985), pp. 42-45.

44. See Kim A. Lawton, "A Clean Sweep for Religious Groups," *Christianity Today,* 12 August 1988, p. 54 (*Bowen* v. *Kendrick* [1988]).

45. Abraham, "Religion, Constitution, Court, and Society," p. 18.

A State may lend to parochial school children geography textbooks that contain maps of the United States for use in a geography class, but the State may not lend maps of the United States for use in a geography class. A State may lend textbooks on American colonial history, but may not lend a film on George Washington, or a film projector to show it in history class.

These are but two of eight such contradictions listed, several of which we have noted earlier.[46] There were, according to a listing compiled by Henry J. Abraham, sixteen Supreme Court decisions concerning aid to nonpublic schools between 1970 and 1986 that collectively illustrate the lack of any kind of consistency.[47]

In 1963 the Supreme Court in *Abington School District* v. *Schempp* outlawed Pennsylvania's long-required morning reading of ten verses from the King James Version of the Bible.[48] The courts continued to follow this vein until 1985 when in *Wallace* v. *Jaffree* they refused to permit a moment of meditation or silent prayer. The inclusion of the words *silent prayer* seems to have been the kicker; there is widespread belief that another court would sustain a moment of silent meditation without any reference to prayer.[49] Such a scenario appeared likely when an appeal on behalf of a New Jersey law that would have permitted "students to observe a minute of silence . . . 'for quiet and private contemplation and introspection'" was brought before the Court, the law having been declared unconstitutional in the lower federal courts. However, in *Karcher, Speaker of the New Jersey General Assembly, et al.* v. *May et al.* (1987), the Court avoided the issue by ruling that because the parties who had brought the appeal, the presiding officers of the New Jersey Assembly and Senate, had lost their offices, and because

46. *Wallace* v. *Jaffree,* 472 U.S. 38 (1985); reprinted as "The True Meaning of the Establishment Clause: A Dissent," in *How Does the Constitution . . .* , ed. Goldwin and Kaufman, pp. 99-113, quote on p. 111.

47. Abraham, "Religion, Constitution, Court, and Society," p. 28.

48. *Abington School District* v. *Schempp,* 374 U.S. 203 (1963).

49. See Abraham, "Religion, Constitution, Court, and Society," p. 38.

their successors were withdrawing the appeal, "that withdrawal left the Court without a case or controversy."[50]

Another aspect of the prayer issue arose when a United States circuit court in January of 1989 outlawed the "organized prayer" that was virtually a universal feature of southern high school football games.[51] On May 30, 1989, the Supreme Court rejected an appeal, which allowed the lower court's ruling to stand.[52] With the onset of the 1989 football season, there were numerous examples of acts of defiance against the ruling, and it has been parodied in the Tank McNamera comic strip.

Another area of church-state concern has to do with the displays of Christmas nativity scenes and Hanukkah menorahs on public property. To date, the rule of thumb used by the Court in a Pawtucket, Rhode Island, case seems to be if the cost involved is trivial, there is no violation of the First Amendment.[53] In 1988, the Third Circuit Court of Appeals, in response to suits brought by the ACLU, barred both a nativity scene and a menorah on public property. This Pittsburgh ruling had opened the opportunity for a future reconsideration by the high court, particularly as other federal judiciaries have been, in the words of an ACLU spokesman, "schizophrenic on the issue."[54] A subsequent ruling, *County of Allegheny* v. *American Civil Liberties Union, Greater Pittsburgh Chapter*, has done nothing to clarify the issues.[55]

---

50. Slip Opinion, 85-1551, "Syllabus," 1 (argued Oct. 6, 1987, decided Dec. 1, 1987).

51. *Douglas County School District* v. *Doug Jager and William Jager*, 862 F2d 824 (1989).

52. *Memorandum decision*, 109 S. Ct. (1989), p. 2431.

53. See *Lynch* v. *Donnelly*, 465 U.S. 668 (1987). This appeal was upheld by a 4-4 vote.

54. "Revisiting the Reindeer Rule," *Time*, 12 December 1988, p. 71.

55. 109 S. Ct. 3086 (1989).

V. Continuing and Future Problems

There is every expectation that challenges will continue in the areas of tax exemption and the references to God in the Pledge of Allegiance and on the nation's currency. Strict separationist Leonard W. Levy, however, suggests that "suits brought by the ACLU to have courts hold unconstitutional every cooperative relationship between government and religion can damage the cause of separation by making it look over-rigid and ridiculous."[56] For many, however, the support of military and other chaplains along with the ceremonial inclusion of invocations, benedictions, and the use of religious symbols violates the Constitution.[57] That such issues are still current is illustrated by an Associated Press release, dated Monday, September 18, 1989, announcing that the New Jersey Division of Taxation had decided to "lift the tax exemption on Bibles and other religious Scriptures." Their action was based on a Supreme Court ruling of the previous February that struck down a Texas sales tax exemption specifically for religious literature marketed by a profit-making publisher.[58]

The other end of the spectrum was illustrated in 1984, in the case of *Grove City v. Bell*. The president of the religiously oriented, small liberal arts college charged that "the government claimed jurisdiction over Grove City College even though it received no federal funds." The rationale was that the 400 students (of 2,200) who received federal tuition grants did so as individuals. In March 1988, Congress passed the Civil Rights Restoration Act, also known as the "Grove City Bill," the thrust of which is that if an institution receives a single dollar of federal aid, "the entire institution must comply with far-reaching anti-discrimination rules."[59]

In another case involving a college, tax exemption has been

56. Levy, *Establishment Clause*, p. 177.

57. For a list of possible vulnerable areas, see Pfeffer, *Church, State and Freedom*, pp. 168-71.

58. *Trenton Times*, 18 September 1989; *Texas Monthly, Inc. v. Bob Bullock, Comptroller of Accounts for the State of Texas*, 109 S. Ct. 890 (1989).

59. Charles S. Mackenzie, "Just Say No to Uncle Sam's Money," *Christianity Today*, 2 September 1988, p. 12.

denied Bob Jones University because of its racial policies that forbid student interracial dating and marriage. Chief Justice Burger wrote that the public interest in "eradicating racial discrimination in education substantially outweighs whatever burden denial of tax benefits places on the petitioners' exercise of their religious beliefs."[60] Further, the federal courts, in protecting minority rights, have forced Georgetown University, against its religious values and beliefs, to recognize and provide institutional support to a minority organization of "Gays" committed to public espousal and even proselytizing of a deviant life-style. The order freed them from any jeopardy related to any institutional regulation or discipline for private practice of their life-style. After eight years of litigations and reversals, the university has surrendered, causing religious critics to question whether religious freedoms have been subordinated to other "rights."[61]

In 1988 the high court ruled 8-1 to suspend a $50,000 fine assessed by a lower court because the Catholic Church had refused to furnish court-subpoenaed documents that were demanded in a case brought in an effort to deny the Catholic Church its tax-exempt status. A complicated case, it produced a not necessarily definitive decision; Justice Kennedy for the majority questioned the status of the party bringing suit and then noted cryptically that "in a free society . . . courts have finite bounds of authority."[62] The dimension of the support for parochial education has to be a concern for champions of the public school who philosophically still believe in the democratic tradition of equality and retain a fixed article of faith that public education constitutes a great democratic homogenizing

60. *Bob Jones University* v. *United States* and *Goldsboro Christian Schools* v. *United States,* 397 U.S. 574 (1983), quoted in A. James Reichley, *Religion in American Public Life* (Washington, D.C.: The Brookings Institution, 1985), p. 154.

61. James Kilpatrick, "Protecting Religion Against State Intrusion," *Trenton (N.J.) Times,* 27 August 1988, Op-Ed page; Charles Colson, "A Remedy for Christian 'Homophobia': Coercive Enlightenment," *Christianity Today,* 15 July 1988, p. 72; "Everything Goes under 'Civil Rights,'" *National Review,* 13 May 1988, p. 69.

62. Lawton, "Clean Sweep," p. 54; *U.S. Catholic Conference* v. *Abortion Rights Mobilization (ARM).*

agency. However, the failure of government in many areas, particularly in education, produces sympathy for those who opt for the nonpublic school as a feasible option. And the question still remains as to whether nonpublic education is a privilege that should be supported by the user or a right to be subsidized by the public.

Possibly the greatest divisive issue in modern American society is that of abortion. I find little prospect of any solution, let alone reason, justice, or right, in the arguments of either the pro-life or the freedom of choice proponents who are committed to moral and ideological absolutes. A reasonable position that might be maintained in the face of attacks from both sides is, at least from this perspective, a pragmatic compromise based on majority desires, which must not force precipitous decisions on the pregnant individual. It is to be hoped that some compromise can be discovered that will consider the health of our society as well as the needs of the unfortunate female. Perhaps no case since the Dred Scott decision has stirred so much emotion as has *Roe* v. *Wade,* and it appears probable that the decision may be reversed in the future.[63] Apparently, this decision has satisfied no one, and unfortunately any effort to satisfy any party may be an exercise in futility as new advances in medicine and medical technology offer awesome potentialities for the future. Certainly these advances raise new issues in abortion practices as well as in the highly controversial "right to die" area.[64] It is worth noting that the reversal of *Roe* v. *Wade* would not outlaw abortion but would return decisionmaking to the states and possibly to Congress.[65] Havoc is marring both political elective contests and the ordinary business of state legislatures as many issues are being subordinated to the pro-choice/pro-life tug-of-war.

On occasion the justices have been their own most reveal-

63. 410 U.S. 152 (1973); for a meaningful discussion one might examine Gene Sperling, "Justice in the Middle," *Atlantic,* March 1988, pp. 26-33.

64. For detailed examinations of the question of abortion, see Cox, *Court and Constitution,* pp. 322-38, 347, and David A. Richards, *Toleration and the Constitution* (New York: Oxford Univ. Press, 1986), pp. 261-69.

65. *Webster* v. *Reproductive Health Services,* 109 S. Ct. 3040 (1989).

ing critics. For example, Justice Black in his dissent in *Harper* v. *Virginia Board of Elections*[66] chastised his fellow justices for using the Equal Protection Clause to permit the Court "to write into the Constitution its notions of what it thinks is good government policy."[67] On another occasion Justice Byron "Whizzer" White, with suprising candor, opined that the justices have "carved out what they deemed to be the most desirable national policy governing various aspects of the church-state relationships."[68]

One of the devices of the stand-up comic is the old line "I've got good news and I've got bad news." We can borrow this lead-in to speculate about our constitutional future. The good news is that despite differences, we have achieved an acceptable religious pluralism along with an accomplished separation of church and state that has allowed for a pluralistic society capable of permitting "many chambers" in a single "house." The two-hundred-year track record validates this, at least externally. The bad news is the picture conjured up by our worst possible scenario—a fragmented society whose fragments have become so diverse that they repel one another rather than attract or meld.

Part of the problem lies in the fact that constitutional theorists, including judges, relegate the constitutional consideration of religion to a textual examination of the wording of the No Test Clause in the main body of the Constitution and then the specific language of the No Establishment and Free Exercise clauses of the First Amendment. They largely limit further consideration to the debates of the Constitutional Convention and of the First Congress, plus the language of Virginia's Statute of Religious Freedom and of Madison's *Memorial and Remonstrance,* supplemented by a passing reference to Jefferson's "wall of separation." Then, largely without considering the context, jurists perform an exegesis that rivals the biblical documentation of the fundamentalists and then—once the pronouncement is made, regardless of the validity of the documentation, and relying on

---

66. 383 U.S. 663-676 (1966).
67. Quoted in Cox, *Court and Constitution,* p. 342.
68. Quoted in Bradley, *Church-State Relationships,* p. 144.

the principle of *stare decisis*—they proceed, on the assumption that the pronouncement validates the precedent. It would appear that most of the problems of contemporary constitutional interpretation and judicial decision lie in the fact that, according to most commentators, there has been no consistency.

On a slightly different tack, Peter Berger quotes Thomas J. Curry's judgment that as the first Congress considered the First Amendment, it "approached the subject in a somewhat hasty and absentminded manner." Further, according to Curry, to judge the language of the debate and of the amendment "as a carefully worded analysis of church-state relations would be to overburden" it. Therefore, suggests Berger (perhaps not inaccurately), "This is an historian's judgement. It goes without saying that lawyers and constitutional theorists are not likely to be much restrained by it: overburdening texts is their vocation."[69]

Archibald Cox describes what he sees as two judicial stances. "One extreme view," he says, "views the Court as a political body actually and properly engaged in pursuing policy goals, even though somewhat limited by jurisdictional rules and by the tradition of cloaking judicial policy making in the concepts of the legal profession." This view has been labeled "activist" and has been said to "politicize the process of constitutional interpretation." In contraposition are those who are more attracted to the principle of "judicial restraint" or "judicial conservatism," which Cox notes does not mean political conservatism. They emphasize representative self-government, majority rule, and the importance of the federal system and look askance at the use of "vague constitutional phrases" to set aside state laws and local ordinances. In addition, they express a great respect for the body of the law accumulated step by step throughout the nation's history and are concerned at the seemingly frivolous setting aside of long-held principles, sometimes by a single judge. Further, they feel that the judgments and orders of the Su-

69. Peter L. Berger, "Religion in Post-Protestant America," *Commentary,* May 1986, pp. 41-45, reprinted in *Religion in American Life,* ed. Podell, pp. 27-39, quote on pp. 28-29.

preme Court need to be limited so that they do not intrude on the preserves of the Executive and Legislative branches.[70]

Justice Douglas, speaking for the majority, used *Griswold* v. *Connecticut*, a case concerned with the distribution of contraceptives, to testify to "a right to privacy older than the Bill of Rights—older than our political parties, older than our school system." Justice Black dissented, denying that the Bill of Rights included a "right to Privacy"; he questioned the notion that it was

> the duty of this Court to keep the Constitution in tune with the times. . . . The Constitution makers knew the need for change and provided for it. Amendments suggested by the people's elected representatives can be submitted to the people or their selected agents for ratification.[71]

Elsewhere in this volume Leo Pfeffer has categorized the four groups that are most concerned with church-state relations. First he lists the absolute separationists and then two groups who are opposed to strict separation, the accomodationists who want public resources applied to varying degrees to parochial education and the fundamentalists who are particularly concerned with their tax-exempt status for their schools as well as for their places of worship, followed by the final group, who are concerned about those who in their opposition to the cults have ridden rough-shod over the Constitution to achieve courtroom victories characterized by excessive fines awarded by juries in a manner that often seems to be in violation of the Free Exercise Clause.[72]

Harvey Cox has noted that in order to get a true prospective one must comprehend the rebirth of American religious commitment that is taking place and see this in a broader world perspective—particularly in terms of the growth of fundamentalism and the threat of cults, not just in America but worldwide. One could also note the invasion of oriental religions and mystical occults. Indeed, it might be useful to place the more

70. Cox, *Court and Constitution*, p. 349.
71. *Griswold* v. *Connecticut*, 381 U.S. 479 (1965).
72. See Pfeffer's essay in this volume.

extreme varieties of "secular humanism" among the cults.[73] R. Laurence Moore has expressed his concern "about emphases in past scholarship that have encouraged misinterpretation of the contemporary religious scene." There is not a period of American history, he notes, when "so-called small sects" were not increasing their membership at a greater rate than were the entrenched mainstream denominations. He further notes that these "groups," whether they were evangelicals of the Great Awakening or Moonies, have caused religious concern and have always challenged existing vested interests.[74]

VI. Critics

Philosopher Robert Paul Wolff has provided a cynical evaluation of modern "pluralism." According to Wolff, the theories of "democratic pluralism" "grew out of nineteenth-century attacks on the methodological individualism of the classical liberal tradition."[75]

Michael Kammen perceptively notes that until the late nineteenth century, "States' rights received far more attention than civil rights in general or the Bill of Rights in particular."[76]

The often contradictory and persistently activist decisions

---

73. For discussions of "Secular Humanism" see Harvey Cox and Leo Pfeffer in this volume; see also Pfeffer, "How Religious Is Secular Humanism?" *The Humanist* 47 (Sept./Oct. 1988): 13-18, 50; Paul Kurtz, *In Defense of Secular Humanism* (Buffalo: Prometheus Books, 1983); Neuhaus, "What the Fundamentalists Want," pp. 222-35.

74. R. Laurence Moore, *Religious Outsiders and the Making of Americans* (New York: Oxford Univ. Press, 1986), p. x; Thomas Robbins, "Marginal Movements," *Society* 21 (May/June 1984), reprinted in *Religion in American Life*, ed. Podell, pp. 179-92; also Robbins, "New Religious Movements on the Frontier of Church and State," in *Cults, Culture and the Law: Perspectives on New Religious Movements*, ed. Thomas Robbins, William C. Shepherd, and James McBride (Chico, Calif.: Scholars Press, 1985), pp. 7-27.

75. Robert Paul Wolff, "Beyond Tolerance," in *A Critique of Pure Tolerance*, ed. Robert Paul Wolff, R. Barrington Moore, and Herbert Marcuse (Boston: Beacon Press, 1965), p. 5.

76. Kammen, *A Machine That Would Go of Itself*, p. 188.

of the Supreme Court have in many ways polarized the Christian community between traditionalists who find the invasion of their long-held values to be unjustified by any constitutional rationale and those members of the community who find judicial activism necessary and appropriate to sustain the human rights of privacy, economic justice, and gender that have been extrapolated from constitutional generalities.[77]

One problem seems to be that many thoughtful Christians are concerned by their perceptions of the way affairs have developed. Religious conservative William A. Stanmeyer seems to be speaking for many of them when he calls our society "Post-Christian America." He begins one chapter of his book with the words, "The Secular State grows more hostile to Christianity," and contends that as the

> Secularists seek to gain control of the organs of public policy, the secular humanists will attack the enclaves of Christian communal life, such as schools, hospitals, and other charitable organizations transfused with religious commitment. Their goal is to reduce Christian influence on public morality to the most token and accidental sort.[78]

The result would be what Richard John Neuhaus calls the "naked public square," a place where public life has been completely secularized and where "free exercise" of religion has been denied.[79]

Not everyone sees it this way, however. An ACLU solicit-

77. William A. Stanmeyer, *Clear and Present Danger: Church and State in Post Christian America* (Ann Arbor: Servant Publications, 1983).

78. Stanmeyer, *Clear and Present Danger,* pp. 5, 15. The term *Post Christian* was not original with Stanmeyer; see Gabriel Vahanian, *The Death of God: The Culture of Our Post-Christian Era* (1961), cited in Sydney E. Alstrom, "The Moral and Theological Revolution of the 1960's and Its Implications for American Religious History," in *The State of American History,* ed. Herbert J. Bass (Chicago: Quadrangle Books, 1970), pp. 98-118.

79. Richard John Neuhaus, *The Naked Public Square* (Grand Rapids: Eerdmans, 1984); see also Berger, "Religion in Post-Protestant America," p. 33. The recent Supreme Court decision granting "dial-a-porn" protection under the First Amendment adds to the ire of religious conservatives; *Sable Communications of California, Inc.* v. *Federal Communication Commission,* 109 S. Ct. 2829 (1989).

ing letter states that the Moral Majority "want their religious doctrines enacted into law and imposed on everybody."[80]

A most ominous portent upon the horizon seems to be a revolutionary philosophical reorientation that has taken place in areas of our intellectual community. William N. Sullivan writes in *Habits of the Heart* that "modern individualism seems to be producing a way of life that is neither individually nor socially viable." We have, according to Bellah and his associates, committed the cardinal sin: "we have put our own good, as individuals, as groups, as a nation, ahead of the common good."[81] Steven M. Tipton has discovered that "utilitarian culture grew away from biblical morality in a modernizing America." Sullivan rejects "finding a way to transcend conceptually a purely utilitarian understanding of politics and a way to challenge the domination of social relationships by bureaucratic management and the workings of capitalistic economics."[82]

Does the attack on the individual and his freedom, a concept so important to the Framers, somehow equate selfishness and callous self-seeking? Is it possible that today's efforts to use the courts to bypass legislative decisions are somehow elitist and antimajoritarian? Is this today's equivalent of the eighteenth-century anti-Federalists? Douglass Adair, following Cecilia Kenyon's characterization of the anti-Federalists as "Men of Little Faith," notes that their opposition to the Constitution was antimajoritarian and antidemocratic. One might ask if today's judicial activists are the intellectual descendants of the opponents of the Constitution of the 1780s.[83]

80. Quoted in Stanmeyer, *Clear and Present Danger*, p. 29.

81. Robert N. Bellah et al., *Habits of the Heart: Individualism and Commitment in American Life* (San Francisco: Harper & Row, 1985), pp. 144, 285; see also p. 294.

82. Bellah et al., *Individualism and Commitment*, pp. 351, 394; cf. pp. 392-99.

83. Douglass G. Adair, "'Experience Must Be Our Only Guide': History, Democratic Theory, and the United States Constitution," in *The Reinterpretation of Early American History: Essays in Honor of John Edwin Pomfret*, ed. Ray A. Billington (San Marino, Calif.: Huntington Library, 1966), pp. 129-49; Cecilia Kenyon, "Men of Little Faith: The Anti-Federalists on the Nature of Representative Government," *William and Mary Quarterly*, 3d series, 12 (1955): 3-43.

The dispute over constitutional interpretation is by no means an anti-intellectual versus intellectual issue nor a progressive versus a reactionary one. Unfortunately the persisting conflicts have the result of creating attitudes focusing on "us" and "them," the "them" only too often being the government, the attitude in each camp depending upon whose ox was gored. Maybe we should reexamine our inclinations and seek some "just" accommodation in our constitutional interpretations. One might suggest that finding joy in gloating over moral besting of equally sincere opponents in the public arena is un-Christian. As Reinhold Niebuhr noted, "Our capacity for justice makes democracy possible, but our inclination for injustice makes democracy necessary."[84]

The adversarial approach seems to dominate in modern society. A technique that seems to be on the rise is to identify the proponent of any variant position with supposedly pejorative labels such as "born again," "televangelical," and "Moral Majority," on the one hand and the negative innuendos of "liberal" on the other. Leonard W. Levy, who on many occasions has been the object of attack by the religious accomodationists and the fundamentalists and who has not been remiss in entering the lists, has paid his respect to the importance of tradition and reason as he opines,

> Americans ought to bear in mind that forbearance is sometimes better than disputation or litigation. They should realize that a faulty political compromise may be better than judicial dictation, which does not satisfy the loser and can corrupt the spirit of the victor.[85]

One hopes that reasonable people can regain a set of shared aspirations such as those that Max Stackhouse is calling for with his suggestion that we should revive the ideals expressed in the Declaration of Independence.[86] Only if we can revive a sense of loyalty to the nation and commit ourselves to a constitutional

---

84. Quoted by Jorge Lara-Braud, "Where Faith and the Constitution Converge and Diverge," *Pacific Theological Review* 21 (Spring 1988): 75-80, quote on p. 77.
85. Levy, *Establishment Clause*, p. 179.
86. See Stackhouse's essay in this volume.

system that will subordinate special causes, regardless of their often strongly expressed moral overtones, can we reach working solutions that will provide for a rich and useful future.

VII. Prospects for the Future

The Williamsburg Charter, created in 1988 to memorialize the bicentennial of Virginia's ratification of the Constitution, is a twenty-three-page document produced by the First Liberty Summit, a meeting of several hundred people. Their goal was to produce a document that "hails 'the genius of the First Amendment' while making assertions on the 'place of religion in American life' and on how people of differing faiths (and of no faith) 'contend with each other's deepest differences in the public sphere.'" They expressed a need for a "common vision [that] must embrace a shared understanding of the place of religion in public life and of the guiding principles by which people with deep religious differences can contend robustly but civilly with each other." The numerous signers included many national figures, one of whom was a 1988 Democratic candidate for president; but the document still awaits the signatures of Reagan and Bush as well as the representatives of both the religious right and the ACLU, who have denied it their signatures.[87]

But in the face of these efforts at conciliation, fears still exist. That they underlie constitutional developments was well illustrated in the June 1988 hearings held by the Assembly State Government Committee of the New Jersey legislature. Once again this committee was considering the call for a Constitutional Convention for the purposes of introducing a balanced budget amendment. New Jersey would be the thirty-third state to make the call, although several states have rescinded their call and the status of these is questionable. Proponents insist that the call can be limited to the single charge, but numerous authorities protest

87. Kim A. Lawton, "Out of Many, One—Almost," *Christianity Today,* 12 August 1988, pp. 50-51.

that there is no way that such a body, initiated under the provisions of Article V of the Constitution, can be in any way limited. Testimony was taken and liberal Democratic spokesmen such as former governor and former New Jersey chief justice Richard Hughes challenged the proponents, asking, "Suppose we're wrong?" What irretrievable damage could be done to the Constitution?[88] Among those who followed Hughes was Phyllis Schlafly, spokeswoman for the conservative accomodationists and for the pro-life extremists. Schlafly likewise opposed a constitutional convention and expressed fears of the damage inherent in a convention with the possibility of its being manipulated by special interest groups. She pointedly noted that there is no popular movement for such a convention, and that this call came largely from a Reagan administration that apparently sincerely thought that such a convention could be limited by a charge to consider only a balanced budget amendment.[89] A member of the committee has expressed privately to me his surprise that so many different groups were sincerely concerned.

Perhaps sociologist E. Digby Baltzell comes close to home with his characterization, in another context, of our age: "After all," he said, "ideological purity has always replaced personal morality in revolutionary ages; perhaps personal morality depends on the existence of a certain degree of social order." Does this hold true for our world, which is faced with so many disturbing problems and moral dilemmas? Perhaps it is a revolutionary age; certainly it is a confusing one, and perhaps, this describes the nature of our unsettled arena.[90]

88. *Public Hearings before the Assembly State Government Committee . . .* , 20 June 1988, Trenton, N.J., p. 34; for an analysis of the questions involved, see *Proposed Procedures for a Limited Constitutional Convention: 1984, 98th Congress, 2d Session* (Washington, D.C.: American Enterprise Institute for Public Policy Research, 1984).

89. *Public Hearings,* Schlafly testimony, pp. 40-46, also Appendix, pp. 10x-21x; for support, see Congressman James A. Courtnew (N.J.), Lance Lamberton, and Dr. Beryl Sprinkel, Chairman, President's Council of Economic Advisors, pp. 6-31.

90. E. Digby Baltzell, "The WASP's Last Gasp," *Philadelphia Magazine,* 89 (September 1988): 184-88, quote on p. 188.

Bibliographical Suggestions

The subject of church and state, the First Amendment, and rights is extremely complicated and involves so many disciplines and schools of thought as to make it almost impossible to come up with a few readings that cover the multitudinous range of problems and implications and at the same time do justice to the various moral, political, and ideological positions. Possibly two of the best sources that would enable one to get an initial handle on the problems would be the collections by Robert A. Goldwin and Art Kaufman, eds., *How Does the Constitution Protect Religious Freedom?* (Washington, D.C.: American Enterprise Institute for Public Policy Research, 1988) and by Janet Podell, ed., *Religion in American Life,* The Reference Shelf, vol. 59, no. 5 (New York: H. W. Wilson, 1987). The reader should be warned that both of these are skewed towards the conservative, fundamentalist, or accomodationist viewpoint. To balance these one could read the works (listed below) of Leo Pfeffer or Leonard W. Levy for an essentially secular approach, and Robert L. Maddox's *Separation of Church and State: Guarantor of Religious Freedom* (New York: Crossroad, 1987) for a religious "liberal" view.

Current and recent Supreme Court decisions in their entirety may be found in *West's Supreme Court Reporter* which reached volume 109 in 1989. The texts of the most significant historical cases can be found along with some commentary in Robert S. Alley, *The Supreme Court on Church and State* (New York: Oxford Univ. Press, 1988).

In the realm of constitutional history, Henry J. Abraham's *Freedom and the Court: Civil Rights and Liberties in the United States*, 5th ed. (New York: Oxford Univ. Press, 1988) and Kermit L. Hall's *The Magic Mirror: Law in American History* (New York: Oxford Univ. Press, 1989) are reasonably objective and not characterized by excessive partisanship. But these are just two suggestions out of innumerable possibilities that continue to pour off the presses.

Possibly the most objective of the "fundamentalist" statements is that of William A. Stanmeyer, *Clear and Present Danger: Church and State in Post Christian America* (Ann Arbor: Servant Publications, 1983). Also informative are Gerard V. Bradley, *Church-State Relationships in America* (Westport, Conn.: Greenwood Press, 1987); Robert L. Cord, *Separation of Church and State: Historical Fact and Current Fiction* (New York: Lambeth Press, 1982); and A. James Reichley, *Religion in American Public Life* (Washington, D.C.: The Brookings Institution, 1985). Other conservative spokesmen worthy of notice are Peter Berger, Raoul Berger, Richard John Neuhaus, James McClelland, and Dean Kelley, references to whom will be found in the two collections cited above.

For balancing spokesmen of the liberal school—in addition to Pfeffer, Levy, and Maddox noted above—see the works by Wilbur Edel, Herman Schwartz, and Mark Silk.

The massive extent of the pertinent materials and their comparted nature, which makes comprehensive examination almost impossible, was brought home to the preparer of this bibliographical offering with the discovery of Mark Tushnet's *Red, White and Blue: A Critical Analysis of Constitutional Law* (Cambridge, Mass.: Harvard Univ. Press, 1988), which includes an incisive and comprehensive analysis of the religious dimension based very heavily on the literature found in law school reviews and on the cases themselves, but with only passing references to the literature which (along with actual cases) is the basis for most of the other works cited in this bibliography. The works cited below constitute an attempt to list works across the political-ideological spectrum. Wherever possible, works cited are those with the most recent copyrights, and a rough attempt has been made to classify them.

Works on the Founding Fathers

Alley, Robert, ed. *James Madison on Religious Liberty.* Buffalo: Prometheus Books, 1985.

Bonomi, Patricia U. *Under the Cope of Heaven: Religion, Society and Politics in Colonial America.* Oxford: Oxford Univ. Press, 1986.

Curry, Thomas J. *The First Freedoms: Church and State in America to the Passage of the First Amendment.* New York: Oxford Univ. Press, 1986.

Frost, J. William, "Pennsylvania Institutes Religious Liberty." *Pennsylvania Magazine of History and Biography* 112 (1988): 323-47.

Levy, Leonard W. *The Establishment Clause: Religion and the First Amendment.* New York: Macmillan, 1986.

Levy, Leonard W., ed. *Essays on the Making of the Constitution.* 2d ed. New York: Oxford Univ. Press, 1987.

Levy, Leonard W., and Dennis J. Mahoney. *The Framing and Ratification of the Constitution.* New York: Macmillan, 1987.

McDonald, Forrest. *Novus Ordo Seclorum: The Intellectual Origins of the Constitution.* Lawrence: Univ. Press of Kansas, 1985.

McLoughlin, William G. *Isaac Backus and the American Pietistic Tradition.* Boston: Little, Brown, 1967.

May, Henry F. *The Enlightenment in America.* New York: Oxford Univ. Press, 1976.

Morgan, Edmund S. *Roger Williams: The Church and the State.* New York: W. W. Norton, 1987.

———. *Inventing the People: The Rise of Popular Sovereignty in England and America.* New York: W. W. Norton, 1988.

Rutland, Robert. *James Madison: The Founding Father.* New York: Macmillan, 1987.

Sanford, Charles B. *The Religious Life of Thomas Jefferson.* Charlottesville: Univ. Press of Virginia, 1984.

Storing, Herbert J., ed. *The Anti-Federalist: Writings by the Opponents of the Constitution: An Abridgement by Murray Dry, of The Complete Anti-Federalist.* Chicago: Univ. of Chicago Press, 1985.

General Historical Works

Edel, Wilbur. *Defenders of the Faith: Religion and Politics from Pilgrim Fathers to Ronald Reagan.* New York: Praeger, 1987.

Giffin, Leslie, ed. *Religion and Politics in the American Milieu* (Sponsored by *The Review of Politics* and The Office of Policy Studies, 1986) [Roman Catholic statements].

Handy, Robert T. *A Christian America: Protestant Hopes and Historical Realities.* New York: Oxford Univ. Press, 1971.

Kammen, Michael. *A Machine That Would Go of Itself: The Constitution in American Culture.* New York: Alfred A. Knopf, 1986.

———. *Spheres of Liberty: Changing Perceptions of Liberty in American Culture.* Madison: Univ. of Wisconsin Press, 1986.

Moore, R. Laurence. *Religious Outsiders and the Making of Americans.* New York: Oxford Univ. Press, 1986.

Noll, Mark A., ed. *Religion and American Politics.* New York: Oxford Univ. Press, 1989.

Smith, Page. *The Constitution: A Documentary and Narrative History.* New York: Morrow, 1978.

Wilson, John F., and John M. Mulder. *Religion in American History: Interpretive Essays.* Englewood Cliffs, N.J.: Prentice-Hall, 1978.

General Works on Constitutional Law

Agresto, John. *The Supreme Court and Constitutional Democracy.* Ithaca, N.Y.: Cornell Univ. Press, 1984.

Alley, Robert S. *The Supreme Court on Church and State.* New York: Oxford Univ. Press, 1988.

Cox, Archibald. *The Court and the Constitution.* Boston: Houghton Mifflin, 1987.

Lee, Francis Graham. *Wall of Controversy: Church-State Conflict in America, the Justices and Their Opinions.* Melbourne, Fla.: Robert E. Krieger, 1986.

Katz, Stanley N. "The Strange Birth and Unlikely History of Constitutional Equality." *Journal of American History* 75 (Dec. 1988): 747-62.

O'Brien, David M. *Storm Center: The Supreme Court in American Politics.* New York: W. W. Norton, 1986.

Pfeffer, Leo. *Church, State and Freedom.* Rev. ed. Boston: Beacon Press, 1967.

————. *Religion, State and the Burger Court.* Buffalo: Prometheus Books, 1985.

Stokes, Anson Phelps, and Leo Pfeffer. *Church and State in the United States.* Rev. ed. New York: Harper & Row, 1964.

Other Works Worthy of Note

Ausmus, Harry J. *Will Herberg: From Right to Right.* Chapel Hill: Univ. of North Carolina Press, 1987.

Bellah, Robert N., et al. *Habits of the Heart: Individualism and Commitment in American Life.* San Francisco: Harper & Row, 1986.

Bellah, Robert N., et al., eds. *Individualism and Commitment in American Life: Readings on the Themes of Habits of the Heart.* San Francisco: Harper & Row, 1987.

Hertzke, Allen D. *Representing God in Washington: The Role of Religious Lobbies in the American Polity.* Knoxville: Univ. of Tennessee Press, 1988.

Levinson, Sanford. *Constitutional Faith*. Princeton: Princeton Univ. Press, 1988.

Miller, William L. *The First Liberty: Religion and the American Republic*. New York: Alfred A. Knopf, 1986.

Richards, David A. *Toleration and the Constitution*. New York: Oxford Univ. Press, 1986.

Schwartz, Herman. *Packing the Courts: The Conservatives' Campaign to Rewrite the Constitution*. New York: Charles Scribner's Sons, 1988 [a criticism of right-wing constitutional interpretations].

Silk, Mark. *Spiritual Politics: Religion and America Since World War II*. New York: Simon & Schuster, 1989.

Conservative/Fundamental/Moral Majority

Morgan, Richard E. *Disabling America: The "Rights Industry" in Our Time*. New York: Basic Books, 1984.

Robbins, Thomas, et al., eds. *Cults, Culture and the Law: Perspectives on New Religious Movements*. Chico, Calif.: Scholars Press, 1985.

Schaeffer, Franky. *Bad News for Modern Man: An Agenda for Christian Activism*. Westchester, Ill.: Crossway Books, 1984.

Abortion

Faux, Marian. *Roe vs. Wade: The Story of the Landmark Supreme Court Decision That Made Abortion Legal* (New York: Macmillan, 1988).

Glendon, Mary A. *Abortion and Divorce in Western Law*. Cambridge, Mass.: Harvard Univ. Press, 1987.

Petchesky, Rosalind P. *Abortion and Woman's Choice: The State, Sexuality and Reproductive Freedom*. Boston: Northeastern Univ. Press, 1984.

Rodman, Hyman, et al. *The Abortion Question*. New York: Columbia Univ. Press, 1987.